Healthful Eating

Healthful Eating

A Cookbook for Those with
Candida, Celiac Disease & Diabetes

Lynette J. Hall

iUniverse, Inc.
New York Lincoln Shanghai

Healthful Eating
A Cookbook for Those with Candida, Celiac Disease & Diabetes

iUniverse books may be ordered through booksellers or by contacting:

iUniverse
2021 Pine Lake Road, Suite 100
Lincoln, NE 68512
www.iuniverse.com
1-800-Authors (1-800-288-4677)

ISBN-13: 978-0-595-40055-3 (pbk)
ISBN-13: 0-595-40055-8 (ebk)
ISBN-10: 978-0-595-84438-8 (pbk)
ISBN-10: 0-595-84438-3 (ebk)

Printed in the United States of America

CONTENTS

FOREWORD

May 20, 2006

Dear Reader,

Ms. Hall's book is a giant leap forward for families who know diet is health. Physicians often overlook the role of diet in the development of disease, sadly nutrition is given little heed in medical school training and to this day is mentioned little. It is an odd idea that health could be sustained without a great deal of attention paid to the diet of the patient a doctor attempts to help. Most physicians find they must study nutrition outside of their formal training and we, you and me and all other concerned members of society, need to get busy and point this out so medical schools change their education process. The wild idea that nutrition has little to do with health must change if we are to alleviate disease. After all, what more could the body need other than an organic diet full of a wide variety of foods, clear water, clean air and exercise. That is the recipe for health for every man, woman and child of any age.

Lynette has applied her skills as a gourmet chef to the problem every person, who wants to address systemic candidiasis and intestinal yeast infections, faces. What do I eat? If I have to limit carbohydrates and certainly all sugars what is left to eat? Lynette's wheat free, dairy free, stevia sweetened recipes are unique and healthful for all of us, yeast infections or not. We will enjoy these recipes for years to come.

If each of us gives a copy of this book to our physicians we will contribute to improving the health of our citizens and your doctors will learn something.

I heartily thank Ms. Hall for her contributions in helping my patients live well and enjoy changing their dietary choices.

Dr. Conrad Maulfair, D. O.
Osteopathic Physician
Topton, PA
www.drmaulfair.com

PREFACE

For the last 5–6 years, I have been battling with my weight. It seemed I literally gained 10 pounds by walking by a bakery. Since I did not have the real answer, the blame was on having gone through the "change" or a "slow metabolism" but year after year, I was feeling physically worse with no seeming rhyme, reason or solution.

My long list of complaints had been "diagnosed", wrongly, as a variety of conditions the worst being Congestive Obstructive Pulmonary Disease (COPD). None of the remedies the doctors tried seemed to work and I always had the nagging feeling their "why" was just not the real solution.

Finally, I met a doctor who properly diagnosed all my symptoms and all are related to Candida overgrowth. Since I have been following the Candida restrictions in my diet, all symptoms have disappeared, including those mimicking COPD.

When first presented with the diet restrictions for Candida my first thought was this is going to be bland and definitely boring. I heard other patients at the clinic express their concerns about what they would be able to eat. Many admitted they did not have a clue how to cook great meals with the restrictions. So many people struggled and some just gave up.

A passion for many years has been gourmet cooking. I have studied America's great cooks, such as Julia Child, and their recipes. I had developed quite a few recipes of my own and catered a few events at my local church. Friends have repeatedly said how they enjoy my cooking and commented, "You should open a restaurant!" Since I had the experience in cooking—and knew I could research the rest—the decision was made. I would do something to help everyone and write a cookbook using my knowledge of food, recipe development and how to convert traditional recipes to meet the dietary restrictions.

As my study of Candida progressed I realized that many Candida suffers also had Celiac disease or wheat sensitivity, so I studied up on that. I gathered all my old recipes and old familiar standards and began the conversion. As stevia substituted for sugar, a realization dawned that diabetics would also benefit from these recipes. My doctor emphasized the use of organically grown foods, organic sources of staples and preparing your own food, so study began on the reasons and science behind that too. All the recipes I had developed and my favorites from over the years were gone through and forbidden ingredients replaced with allowed ones. Sugar became stevia and flours substituted or the recipe changed. Condiment recipes were developed and dessert recipes got special attention.

That is what this cookbook is about, healthy recipes everyone can enjoy and specifically meet the dietary restrictions for those with Candida, Celiac disease and will not kill you with sugar. Best of all they are very tasty—you will actually want to eat them and so will the kids—and relatively simple to prepare. True fast food that is good for you!

To our health!

Lynette J Hall

INTRODUCTION

First, let us all understand what these recipes are dealing with in this cookbook. The following definitions come from www.healthscout.com.

Candida (sometimes referred to as monilia) is a fungus that is normally present on the skin and in mucous membranes. The fungus also can travel through the blood stream and affect the throat, intestines, and heart valves.

People with Candida cannot have foods that contain mold or use mold in the processing, such as mold-ripened cheese. Fungal foods like mushrooms, morels and truffles as well as fermented products, which include miso, soy sauce (shoyu), wine and tempeh. Candida sufferers cannot have sugar, honey, yeast or products containing sugars or yeast, which provide food for the candida.

Celiac disease is a digestive disease that damages the small intestine and interferes with absorption of nutrients from food. People who have celiac disease cannot tolerate a protein called gluten, found in wheat, rye, and barley. When people with celiac disease eat foods containing gluten, their immune system responds by damaging the small intestine.

Gluten is a protein group found in wheat and other flours that forms the structure of bread dough. Gluten is in many foods such as licorice, soy sauce, vinegar, some flavorings, most processed foods and even cold cuts. Prepared products like salad dressings, soups and even stock can contain gluten.

Diabetes is a chronic health condition where the body is unable to produce insulin and properly break down sugar (glucose) in the blood. Symptoms include hunger, thirst, excessive urination, and dehydration and weight loss. The treatment of diabetes requires daily insulin injections, proper nutrition and regular exercise.

Diabetics cannot have starches (pastas, rice, bread, cake, potatoes, corn, etc.), fruit and milk, which are high in carbohydrates. In the body, carbohydrates break down into glucose (sugar).

What I have learned

Investigating food, nutrition and the American diet brought some disturbing facts to light. Today media indoctrinates us and advertisements cause us to think that preparing healthy delicious food cannot be fast. We believe that our busy lifestyles preclude cooking at home where we can control the ingredients and portions of what we eat. An unhealthy diet of high fat, empty carbs and processed foods combined with physical inactivity are contributing factors to becoming overweight or obese, not to mention an entire list of various related diseases.

In 1970 with the invention of super sizing or biggie sizing in the fast-food market is the point of spiking in the weight of the average American according to reports in the February issue of Science Magazine and Nutrition Today.

Marion Nestle points out in her book, *Food Politics,* the food industry now produces 3,800 calories a day for every person in the United States (2,200 to 2,500 would be adequate). There is a 500 calorie-a-day increase since 1970. To burn off the extra 500 calories a 200-pound person would need to do aerobic exercise for approximately 55 minutes, or continuously jog for 33 minutes, every single day.

The addition of high-fructose corn syrup to the foods we eat is a factor that far exceeds the addition of any other food in the American diet. Its consumption has increased more than 1000% between 1970 and 1990, according to the US Department of Agriculture.

Obesity and related diseases like candida, diabetes, heart disease, and high-blood pressure have been on the increase in American society and now the rest of the world is starting to catch up. In the past 20 years, there has been a dramatic increase in obesity and the waistlines of the average American. According to the National Health and Nutrition Examination Survey (NHANES) 64% of American adults are overweight or obese, which is a 14% increase from the period of 1988–1994, a 36% increase over the 1967–1980 survey.

The future is just as bad since approximately 15.5 percent of children, ages 6 to 11, are overweight and 15.3 percent are obese. For children, ages 12 to 19,

15.3 percent are overweight and 15.5 percent are obese-according to the National Obesity website. In the period of 1976 to 1980, seven percent of 6 to 11 year olds were obese and 5 percent of children 12 to 19.

This is a drastic increase by more than 50 percent in just two decades.

The Candida Connection

Americans have become a fast society. Fast food, fast medical fixes with antibiotics, fast paced living with little to no exercise. Scientists estimate that 90% of Americans provide a warm home for this yeast-like parasite called Candida albicans.

Over-utilization of antibiotics, the American diet packed with sugars and carbohydrates and a weakened immune system allow these Candida organisms to overpopulate, invade various organs and tissues and wreak havoc on normal bodily functions. Early symptoms of over-growth include chronic aches and pains, digestive problems, lack of energy, memory loss, depression, foggy thinking and many other conditions wrongly associated with getting older. In many cases, it is actually systemic candidasis. Elson M. Haas, M.D., a Candida researcher, has done one of numerous researches that have found this to be fact.

Candida gains a foothold in the human body through antibiotic use and sugar consumption. Today the American diet is full of high fructose corn syrup and heavy on complex carbohydrates (sugars, breads, cereals, pasta, etc.). Many people have an overall weakened immune system due too the overuse of antibiotics, central nervous system drugs (anti-depressives, tranquillizers, sleeping pills), cortisones, contraceptive pills, anti-ulcer/heartburn drugs, and massive use of dental fillings containing mercury.

Processed foods and convenience foods are more popular and contain large quantities of preservatives and coloring agents. All these factors allow the over-population of the yeast which then begins its invasion into various organs and tissues and wreaks havoc on normal bodily functions. When Candida has morphed into its fungal form, it develops roots and implants them in the intestinal wall. When the yeast is hungry, it feeds itself by sending some toxins to your brain to make you eat. Then they breed and multiply and people can have a panoply of symptoms mimicing other conditions and wrongly associated with getting older.

Celiac disease and Diabetes prevalence

Based on University of Chicago data, 1 in 133 average healthy people have Celiac disease whether they know or not. Proteins in cereal grains are responsible for the development of Celiac disease. According to the Celiac Disease Foundation, the disease may appear at any time in a person's life. There are many triggers, after surgery, viral infection, severe emotional stress, pregnancy or childbirth. Celiac Disease affects many body systems with extremely varied symptoms that often mimic other gastrointestinal disorders.

According to the American Diabetes Association, about 176,500 people aged 20 years or younger have diabetes. Diabetes often goes undiagnosed because the symptoms seem relatively harmless, frequent urination, excessive thirst, unusual weight loss or increased fatigue. Diabetes is a disease in which the body either does not produce insulin or does not use it properly. When glucose builds up in the blood instead of going into cells, it can starve cells for energy. Over time, high glucose levels may damage organs and body systems, including the eyes, kidneys, nerves and heart. Type 1 diabetes primarily strikes children and young adults, accounting for 5 to 10% of all diagnosed cases. Type 2 diabetes accounts for 90 to 95% of all diagnosed cases of diabetes. Nutrition is important for good diabetes control. By eating well-balanced meals in the correct amounts, you can keep your blood glucose level as close to normal (non-diabetes level) as possible.

"Great, we are all sick", you might say. Maybe, but we can get healthy again. So what do we do? Well, we learn to eat healthier and prepare our own food. When this journey began, I was greatly surprised what I was actually eating. I thought I was making decent healthy choices for the most part, but reading the labels of items in my cabinets revealed that assumption as wrong. It is by choosing healthier organic ingredients and controlling portions that we all can help control these diseases without having to resort to drugs. If we also learn how to eat healthy when we are out or while traveling we will create a lifestyle that works all the time.

I can hear the groans now, "I don't have the time to make my own meals". Well, contrary to what you may think, it does not take more time to prepare a nutritious, healthy meal at home. In fact in approximately the time it would take for you to drive and order a fast-food or restaurant take-out meal and bring it home, you can make a great healthy meal that even the children will love.

The type of food you eat does count

All the ingredients and spices in this cookbook are from organic sources whether or not specifically stated in the recipes. Why eat organic? Well you would not put contaminated gasoline in your car, would you? Certainly not, it would clog the lines and cause your engine not to run. You should not be putting contaminated food in your body's engine either.

Robert Rodale, editor of Organic Gardening and Farming, first stated the most accepted definition of organic food.

"Food grown without pesticides; grown without artificial fertilizers; grown in soil whose humus content is increased by the additions of organic matter, grown in soil whose mineral content is increased by the application of natural mineral fertilizers; has not been treated with preservatives, hormones, antibiotics, etc."

Some people believe that organic foods are not necessarily more nutritious, that the nutrient content of a plant is part of its DNA and wired in. However, there are many studies available that show organically grown foods are more nutritious and they are generally more pure. Unfortunately, because of the prevalent overuse of pesticides and their long life span in the soils and water, even a tomato grown on an organic farm under strict adherence to Robert Rodale's definition above can have traces of pesticide, although it will be a significantly small amount. Tomatoes and 98% of the peaches tested by the USDA in 2002, showed evidence of at least one pesticide. Other contaminated foods over the years include apples, strawberries, and pears and 47% of the produce sampled by the USDA in 2002 had detectable pesticide residues. Organically grown foods definitely do not have a mixture of wash-off resistant pesticides layered all over its skin.

You can be sure that organically grown or raised foods are not genetically engineered (GE) or genetically modified (GMO). Since 1997 corn, peas and papaya are the most genetically engineered foods available today. Also genetically modified is Canola oil, cottonseed oil, potatoes, soybeans, squash and sugar beets.

Bob L. Smith with Doctor's Data of West Chicago conducted a study and found the average concentration of nutrient minerals in organic foods was about twice that of commercial foods and that the average content of toxic metals, aluminum, cadmium, and mercury was lower in organic foods.

Dr. Joseph Cummins, Professor Emeritus of Genetics at the University of Western Ontario warns: "Probably the greatest threat from genetically altered crops is the insertion of modified virus and insect virus genes into crops. It has been shown in the laboratory that genetic recombination will create highly virulent new viruses from such constructions."

In fact, genetically engineered potatoes and corn, now available in the markets, can and do produce their own pesticide. The crops contain a foreign soil bacterial gene called bacillus thuringiensis, or Bt, which creates a toxin. The purpose of the toxin is to kills insects that attack the plant. There is great debate as to the effects on humans of eating genetically modified foods. In Scotland, a scientist found that modified potatoes weakened the immune system of rats.

Genetically modified foods often contain proteins that have never before been part of the human diet. These are proteins from bacteria and viruses and, in the future companies are planning to use new proteins from insects, scorpions and even people.

Organic certified meats and poultry assure you that no antibiotics or growth hormones were used in raising the animals. The food fed to the animals is organically grown and no nitrates are added to the processed meat. Processors to ensure color retention add nitrates. After all red meat will sell, and gray meat will not. However, sodium nitrite reacts with stomach acid and produces nitrosamines. Studies show they cause cancer in animals when consumed in large quantities. If you want to eat processed meat be sure to get uncured products because it usually means harmful chemicals such as nitrates, nitrites, or phosphates were not used in their preparation.

Learn to read labels

One of the best things we can do for ourselves is to read the labels when shopping. It takes just a moment to scan the ingredient list, which is required on all food nowadays, to see if it contains any of the forbidden foods or chemicals. I began doing this in earnest and was amazed how cane sugar was one of the major ingredients in canned turkey chili or high fructose corn syrup in my garlic basil salad dressing! Not to mention the massive quantities of chemical compounds instead of food used in other food items.

When reading a label, listed ingredients are in order of quantity used in the product. Therefore, if the label has five ingredients and the second is high fructose corn syrup (or cane syrup or sugar) then you know there is more sugar than any following ingredients. This can be revealing if the product is a can of chili and the fourth ingredient is meat after corn syrup at number two.

Today American food manufacturers use nearly 3000 direct food additives like butylated hydroxyanisol-BHA (a white, waxy phenolic (benzene) antioxidant used to preserve fats and oils), sodium benzoate (a white crystalline salt used as a food preservative and antiseptic), sodium erythorbate (keeps food from changing color) and carrageen (derived from moss and used as a thickener and stabilizer in processed foods).

A good rule of thumb is if the label contains more than 5–8 ingredients, words that you cannot pronounce or understand find something else. Chances are those extra ingredients or unpronounceable items on the label are not good for your diet or body.

What's it oil about?

Oil is a key component in the diet. Eating a healthy fat (oil) assists the body to eliminate excess fat. Not all oil is the same; in fact, most "typical" oils in the American diet are the worst ones for the body. Some oils cannot tolerate high heat, when heated beyond a certain temperature they break down and develop carcinogenic compounds. There are some oils that can tolerate high heat without causing carcinogenic compounds but are not really known or used by the average American. There is a great variety of allowable oils to add flavors to your food.

Several oils can handle high-heat cooking like sizzling stir-frying and deep-frying. They are Avocado oil, up to 520° F; Almond oil, up to 495° F; and Coconut oil, up to 450° F. High-oleic safflower and sunflower oils are other good oils as well.

All other oils keep at 320 degrees F or less because using them higher increases oxidation, which is just another way to say they go rancid. Butter, which is great for sautéing, when added to an oil will raise the temperature at which the oil can be heated while imparting another layer of flavor. Do not heat nut oils, like almond and walnut, as they lose their flavor and can become bitter. Best use for nut oils is in cold dishes and in salad dressings.

Olive and hazelnut oils are monounsaturated fats, as are high-oleic (fatty acids) safflower and sunflower oils. Eating monounsaturated, oils seem to reduce total blood cholesterol and the "bad" cholesterol levels. These oils are liquid at room temperature and cloud and thicken when chilled. Olive oils are monounsaturated fats, which lower blood cholesterol and maintain HDL, the "good" cholesterol that helps prevent heart disease. Sesame oil is approximately half monounsaturated and half polyunsaturated fatty acids.

Regular safflower and sunflower, walnut, corn and soybean oils are polyunsaturated oils. These oils also reduce total cholesterol and LDL, but they also decrease HDL's positive effects. These oils when exposed to heat are very susceptible to attack by free radicals that contribute to cancer and other chronic diseases. These oils remain liquid whether in or out of the refrigerator.

The method used to extract oil affects the quality for use in the body. Squeezing the seed, grain, or fruit at high pressure makes an expeller-pressed oil. The higher the pressure, the more heat and the temperature can exceed 300 degrees F.

Cold-pressed oil is made by squeezing (expeller-pressed) at low temperatures. Olive oil and sesame oil are really the only oils that can be truly cold-pressed commercially. Cold-pressed oils are the best for the body as they contain minerals, phosphatides, vitamin E, and are high in trace nutrients.

All extracted oils involve some sort of high heat during processing. The cheaper brands of oil, which is most commercial brands, usually use chemical solvents to extract the oil. Oil separation uses hexane, which is a petroleum solvent, followed by boiling to remove the toxic solvent. Then the oil is bleached and deodorized which involves heating it to over 400 degrees F.

Rancid oil has an unpleasant aroma and acrid taste and to avoid rancidity it is best to store all oils in the refrigerator. Additionally, breaking open and adding one capsule of vitamin E to your bottle of oil will help as well. Some oils thicken when refrigerated, but liquefy when they stand at room temperature. Extra-virgin and virgin olive oils keep about a year after opening. Other olive and monounsaturated oils keep well up to eight months; unrefined polyunsaturated oils only about half as long.

A word about cheese

Most cheese making is via a process involving bacteria and use of vinegar. To acidify the milk bacteria is added so the rennet (either an enzyme from a calf's stomach or derived from molds and yeast) will work and to aid in the curing. The only cheese usually allowed are fresh mozzarella, feta and ricotta. These are the only cheeses you will see in this cookbook. Mozzarella uses citrus acid for processing, ricotta uses lemon juice, and feta ripens in salt brine. As in all other foods, get the freshest you can from an organic source.

Condiments

All commercially made condiments we are accustomed to using, catsup, mustard, and mayonnaise are not allowable foods as they contain sugar, vinegar and sometimes wheat. There is no use of vinegar in any of these recipes because to make vinegar they use yeast culture. This is the reason for the Condiments section not normally found in the standard cookbook.

The recipes in this book should be, for the most part, good for all sufferers of Candida, Celiac disease and diabetics. We use no sugar or sugar based foods such as soy sauce, catsup, vinegars or wine. There is no barley, rye flours or seeds. We do not use wheat although a few recipes use Spelt. Although spelt is wheat, some who are gluten sensitive can tolerate spelt on occasion. Notes are in place on these recipes.

Herb Substitutions

Many of the recipes call for fresh herbs, but sometimes you just do not have them available or on hand. You can make substitutions of fresh with dried.

Remember that the essential oils are more concentrated in dried herbs so you use less. If you want to substitute dried herbs in a recipe that calls for fresh the conversion is simple. Use one-third the amount of dried herb for fresh called for in the recipe. A way to do this is to reduce tablespoons to teaspoons; two tablespoons of fresh oregano equals two teaspoons dried. You can make the flavor of a dried herb fresher by combining it with fresh parsley.

If you use a dried herb, add it to the recipe at the beginning of cooking to develop its flavor. If you use a fresh herb, add it at the end because long cooking can destroy its flavor and color.

When you're out…eating

It is not very difficult to maintain the diet restrictions when having to eat out in restaurants. To sweeten foods carry stevia in packets or a small bottle. Ask what ingredients are in any dish that appeals to you on the menu. Always ask that any forbidden foods or items be left out or served on the side. You can even order a sandwich and just eat the meat leaving the bread alone.

You will have the best success if you try to stick to Japanese, Thai, Korean, East Indian, and Chinese food restaurants when you eat out. They tend to use most of the ingredients allowed in your diet. Be aware that in sauces on many ethnic foods can be sugar or fermented ingredients, such as fish sauce. Chinese cooks use oyster sauce which contains wheat and some restaurants still use MSG. Therefore, it is best to ask for ingredients and to request all sauces be on the side.

If you are at a restaurant where nothing on the menu seems to be allowable, you can always request steamed vegetables and fish, or a salad and a broiled chicken breast. If you explain that you are on a restricted diet because of food sensitivities, most restaurants will do what they can to accommodate you.

A final note

In all recipes, although not necessarily stated, all produce, spices, nuts, eggs, milk, meats and poultry are from organic sources. Some of the recipes call for canned goods. The purpose of this cookbook is not to promote any particular brands or manufacturers items. No particular brands are stated, but all canned goods are organic. When choosing ingredients you must read the label to ensure there are not hidden forbidden ingredients. Beans used contain only the beans, water and salt. Canned coconut milk should only have coconut milk and guar gum.

The stevia used is just stevia with no additional additives. Using one of the many stevia formulations with additions to the stevia, we cannot guarantee the taste will be the same. In addition, crushed stevia leaf powder and stevia extract is not an equal substitution. When using stevia in a recipe it is best to put the stevia into a liquid first before adding into dry ingredients or batter. This allows the stevia to dissolve and permeate the dish.

Most recipes do not use salt. According to the American Heart Association, healthy American adults should eat no more than 2,300 milligrams of sodium a day. This is about 1 teaspoon of sodium chloride (salt). One teaspoon of baking soda has 1000 mg sodium. You can add salt, at your discretion, to food after preparation.

APPETIZERS AND SNACKS

ap·pe·tiz·er: a food or drink to stimulate the appetite and usually served before a meal

snack: a light meal, food eaten between regular meals

Appetizers and Snacks

Kasha Tabbouleh

1 cup cooked kasha (whole, coarse, or medium)
Chicken broth to prepare kasha
⅓ cup chopped green onions
15 fresh mint leaves, chopped
¼ cup chopped parsley
1 large tomato, seeded and chopped
1 tablespoon lemon juice
Romaine lettuce or leaves

    For dressing:
    2 cloves garlic, crushed
    3 tablespoons tahini (can be store bought or see condiments)
    ½ cup plain almond milk (see condiments)
    2 tablespoons fresh-squeezed lemon juice
    1 teaspoon toasted sesame oil

Mix all dressing ingredients in a blender or food processor until smooth.

Prepare kasha according to package directions, using chicken broth for liquid.

Combine all ingredients, and sufficient dressing to moisten kasha, about 3–4 tablespoons.

For best flavor, chill at least 2 hours before serving. Place tabbouleh in center of a plate and encircle with lettuce leaves or endive to use as scoops.

Oriental Lettuce Wraps

2 carrots
2 stalk celery
1 large or 2 small broccoli stalks, peeled
3–4 large cauliflower florets

¼ cup fresh bean sprout
1 tablespoon Bragg's amino acids
Bibb or Boston lettuce leaves

Dice carrots, celery, broccoli stalks, and cauliflower and toss with Braggs. Add fresh bean sprouts and toss lightly. Spoon into fresh, washed lettuce leaves and roll cabbage-roll style.

Greek Lettuce Wraps

2 tomatoes
1 medium cucumber
1 small onion
1 garlic clove
2 tablespoons extra virgin or cold pressed olive oil
½ lemon, juiced
2 leaves fresh basil, torn in small pieces
1 small can sliced black olives
½ block fresh feta cheese, crumbled into small pieces
Bibb or Boston lettuce leaves

Dice tomatoes, cucumbers, and onion, add in a little smashed garlic and toss with olive oil and a little lemon juice, add fresh basil.

Spoon into fresh lettuce leaves and add a few good olives and feta. Roll cabbage roll style.

Mexican Wraps

1 15 ½-ounce can of pinto beans, drained
¼ teaspoon cumin
¼ teaspoon chili powder
1 garlic clove
1 large or 2 small Roma tomatoes
Bibb or Boston lettuce leaves

Smash pinto beans with cumin, chili powder, tomato and garlic. Roll tablespoonfuls in fresh lettuce leaves.

Zucchini Rolls

2 zucchini, slice thin lengthwise
1 lemon, juice and zest
2 tablespoons extra virgin or cold pressed olive oil
1 clove of garlic, smashed
1 tablespoon fresh basil, chopped
¼ teaspoon dried oregano
Arugula, washed and dried

In a small bowl, mix together lemon juice, zest, olive oil, garlic, oregano and basil. Pour into a shallow baking pan and layer the zucchini. Marinate 1 hour in refrigerator.

Remove zucchini slices from marinade and place a few arugula leaves in wide end of each zucchini slice. Roll up, pin roll with toothpick.

Tofu "Cheese" Sauce

NOTE: Only use fresh tofu that is stored and sold in brine.

½ pound fresh tofu
1 tablespoon lemon juice
2 cloves garlic, sliced
Water to blend, about 2 tablespoons

Place all ingredients in a blender and process until smooth.

Makes approximately 1 cup

Tomato Cups

1 to 2 packages large cherry tomatoes
½ small cucumber
2 stalks celery
2 green onions
½ cup fresh parsley
1 tablespoon fresh mint

1 clove garlic
½ cup sunflower seeds
1 tablespoon lemon juice
1 tablespoon extra virgin or cold pressed olive oil

Cut cherry tomatoes in half and scoop out center. Add tomato pulp, celery, onions, parsley, garlic, and mint with sunflower seeds, oil and lemon in a food processor or blender and finely chop. Fill tomato halves with mixture.

Spicy Bean Dip

1 15 ½-ounce can organic black beans, drained
1 15 ½-ounce can organic kidney beans, drained
1 teaspoon safflower oil
2 cloves garlic, minced
½ cup chopped onion
½ cup diced tomato
½ cup pico de gallo salsa (see condiments)
½ teaspoon ground cumin
½ teaspoon chili powder
1 tablespoon diced jalapeño pepper
¼ cup mozzarella cheese, coarsely grated
1 tablespoon fresh lime juice

Place beans in a bowl; partially mash until chunky. Heat oil in a frying pan, add onion and garlic; sauté for 4 minutes over medium heat. Add beans, tomato, salsa, cumin, chili powder and pepper.

Cook for 5 minutes or until thick, stirring constantly. Remove from heat and stir in the cheese and lime juice. Stir until well blended and cheese has melted.

Tofu Garlic Cheese

NOTE: Only use fresh tofu that is stored and sold in brine.

1 cup mashed tofu
¼ cup chopped fresh basil
4 cloves garlic

1 tablespoon plus 1½ teaspoons lemon juice
Few flakes of dried red pepper (optional)
Ground black pepper to taste

Wrap tofu in cheesecloth and wring out excess moisture, place in a bowl and mash.

In a blender, combine the garlic and basil, process until moderately fine, add lemon juice, pepper, red pepper flakes and blend.

Add the tofu to mixture in blender and blend until smooth. Pour into a bowl and refrigerate covered for several hours.

Remove from refrigerator, place into parchment paper and shape into a log, chill overnight.

To serve, slice rounds and serve on slices of zucchini or squash.

Spinach Cheese

10½ ounces fresh feta cheese
20 leaves of baby spinach, washed and dried
2 cloves garlic, crushed
1 sprig fresh parsley
1 sprig fresh tarragon
1 tablespoon chives, chopped fine
Pepper to taste

Clean spinach and trim off stalk ends, chop into a fine dice. Place in a bowl with crumbled feta and add garlic. Chop parsley fine and add to bowl along with chopped chives.

Strip the leaves from the sprig of tarragon. If small and fine add to bowl, otherwise chop first. Mix and season with pepper to taste.

Chill in refrigerator for 1 hour.

Serves 4

Shrimp Cocktail

20 chilled large shrimp, peeled with tail on and cleaned
1 cup tomato paste
Dash of cayenne pepper
1 clove garlic, minced
½ teaspoon chili powder
2 tablespoons lemon juice
½ tablespoon fresh grated horseradish (if bought ensure it is just horseradish without vinegar)
¼ teaspoon grated onion
⅓ cup finely chopped parsley

Combine all ingredients except shrimp and mix well.

Place mixture in center of small bowl and line the rim with the shrimp.

Serves 4

Non-dairy Cheese Log

1 can coconut milk (just coconut and guar gum)
1 envelope gelatin
½ cup organic walnuts
½ cup organic almonds
1 cup well cooked organic carrots
2½ teaspoons onion powder
½ teaspoon garlic powder
⅓ cup lemon juice

Blend all ingredients together in a food processor.

Place in a parchment paper and roll into a log, chill for 1 hour in refrigerator.

Remove and roll in chopped nuts, chives or parsley and chill overnight.

Red Pepper Hummus

1 16-ounce can garbanzo beans, drained and rinsed
1 tablespoon extra virgin or cold pressed olive oil
1 medium red bell pepper, cut into ½-inch pieces
1 tablespoon tahini (store bought or see condiments)
1 fresh lime, juiced
1½ tablespoons water
¼ teaspoon ground black pepper
¼ teaspoon garlic powder

In a food processor, mix the garbanzo beans, olive oil, red bell pepper, tahini, limejuice, water, black pepper and garlic powder. Blend until smooth.

Yogurt Cheese Balls

3 cups plain unsweetened yogurt, drained
1 teaspoon cumin seeds
½ tablespoon coriander seeds
Several grinds of fresh black pepper
3–4 tablespoons finely chopped almonds
1 ½ tablespoons sesame seeds

Line a colander with a triple layer of cheesecloth, letting it fall over the sides. Place the colander over a bowl and spoon in the yogurt. Fold the excess cheese-cloth over the top and cover. Drain in the refrigerator for 24–36 hours, or until a thick-curd cheese forms. (Can be made 2–3 days in advance but keep covered and refrigerated).

Place the cumin and coriander seeds in a pan and cook over moderate heat until they darken a few shades. Crush in a mortar with a pestle or grind in a food pro-cessor or spice grinder. Place the spice mixture in a bowl; add the yogurt cheese and pepper. Mix well.

On two different plates place the ground almonds and sesame seeds. Using a mea-suring spoon, scoop approximately ½ tablespoon of yogurt and drop on one of each of the coatings. Carefully roll the balls in the coatings until round and well coated.

Smoked Turkey Asparagus

24 stalks of asparagus
8 slices of organic smoked turkey, thin sliced
1½ teaspoons extra virgin or cold pressed olive oil
24 pieces of green onion tops, dropped in boiling water and removed immediately

Preheat oven to 400 degrees F.

Wash the asparagus. Hold at the tip and the base lightly in two fingers each end. Bend the asparagus in an arch until it snaps. This is the exact point to cut the asparagus. Use the snapped piece, measure against and cut all asparagus to length. Lightly peel the last 1-inch of thick end. Lay asparagus on a shallow baking pan and sprinkle and coat with the olive oil.

Slice each piece of smoked turkey into three strips lengthwise. Wrap a strip of turkey around the asparagus stalk leaving the tips unwrapped. Tie a piece of green onion around the turkey to hold.

Place in oven for 12 minutes.

Serves 4–6

BREADS, WRAPS AND CRACKERS

bread: a usually baked and leavened food made of a mixture whose basic constituent is flour or meal

wrap: round thin cake of unleavened cornmeal or wheat flour bread

cracker: a dry thin crispy baked product either leavened or unleavened

Breads, Wraps and Crackers

Blueberry Almond Muffins

Note: Spelt is wheat; celiac sufferers should not use this recipe. Candida should only eat in rotation when on maintenance.

2 cups spelt flour
1 tablespoon crushed stevia leaf powder
1 rounded teaspoon non-aluminum baking powder
1 teaspoon cinnamon
4 organic eggs, at room temperature
½ cup butter, melted
½ cup canned coconut milk (just coconut milk and guar gum)
1 tablespoon lemon juice
1 teaspoon organic non-alcohol vanilla extract
1 cup blueberries (fresh or frozen)

Preheat the oven to 350 degrees F. Line a muffin tin with liners.

In a medium bowl, mix the eggs, melted butter, lemon juice, vanilla and coconut milk.

In a larger bowl, mix the flour, baking powder, stevia, and cinnamon. Add the wet ingredients and mix until just combined but do not beat. Add the berries and mix again.

Pour into muffin pans and bake for 20–25 minutes. They are done when risen, golden brown and set in the middle. Leave in the pan on a cooling rack for 5 minutes, and then remove to cool completely.

Makes 12

Millet Muffins

Preheat oven to 375 degrees F. Oil muffin tins.

1½ cups organic millet flour
½ cup organic soy flour
1 tablespoon non-aluminum baking powder
¼ teaspoon lemon zest
1 cup water
¼ cup safflower oil
1½ teaspoons crushed stevia leaf powder

Combine all dry ingredients in a medium bowl. Mix liquid ingredients together and add to dry ingredients. Put mixture in well-oiled muffin tins.

Bake for 15–20 minutes or until done.

Makes 12

Batter Bread

Preheat oven to 325 degrees F.

6 tablespoons extra virgin or cold pressed olive oil
⅛ teaspoon crushed stevia leaf powder
3 organic eggs
1 cup pecan nut meal
¼ cup arrowroot powder

Combine all ingredients in a food processor and pour onto a greased cookie sheet.

Bake approximately 15 minutes. Cut into desired pieces.

Chickpea Crackers

1 cup chickpea flour
2 tablespoons arrowroot powder
1 tablespoon extra virgin or cold pressed olive oil
⅓ cup water
⅛ teaspoon salt

Preheat oven to 375 degrees F.

Mix all ingredients together. Add more chickpea flour, a small amount at a time, until dough is dry enough to form into balls without sticking. It should still be slightly wet.

Use a sheet of parchment or wax paper. Sprinkle paper with chickpea flour. Roll dough into small balls and place on paper, sprinkle with flour. Cover with another sheet of paper and squash or roll to about ⅛ inch thick. Place on slightly oiled and floured bake sheet.

Bake approximately ten minutes, until underside of crackers is brown, then flip over and bake until browned on other side.

Variations: chop up some scallions, roast some garlic, or add your favorite spices for different flavors.

Buckwheat Pancakes

Heat and lightly oil a griddle.

¾ cup buckwheat flour
¼ cup millet flour
1 teaspoon non-aluminum baking powder
¾ tablespoon crushed stevia leaf powder
1 organic egg, beaten
¾–1 cup coconut milk
2 tablespoons melted butter

Mix dry ingredients together, add egg, milk, and butter beating well after each addition.

Pour ¼ cup batter for each pancake onto hot griddle. Cook 1 to 1½ minutes, turning when edges look cooked and bubbles begin to break on the surface. Continue to cook 1 to 1½ minutes more or until brown.

Spinach Crepes

½ cup buckwheat flour
1 large organic egg, beaten
1¼ cups organic coconut milk (just coconut milk and guar gum)
4½ ounces frozen spinach, thawed, well drained and squeezed dry and chopped
2 tablespoons safflower oil

Sift flour and add to a bowl. Make a well in the center and add egg. Gradually whisk in the coconut milk and add the spinach. Allow batter to stand for 30 minutes.

Whisk batter. Brush a crepe pan with oil and heat until hot.

Pour in just enough batter to cover pan bottom thinly. Cook for 1–2 minutes until set and then turn over and cook for 1 minute until golden brown.

Makes 8

Cinnamon Arrowroot Bread

½ cup ground almonds
1½ cups arrowroot powder
¾ teaspoon crushed stevia leaf powder
1 organic egg
⅛ cup organic almond nut milk (store bought or see condiments)
½ teaspoon cinnamon

Combine egg and almond milk with ground almonds, arrowroot and mix. If dry add a bit more nut milk slowly until smooth dough forms.

Spread evenly on an oiled cookie sheet and bake in a 350-degree oven for 30 minutes.

Variations: Leave out the cinnamon and add ¼ teaspoon basil and thyme. Spread dough very thinly on cookie sheet and bake to make a cracker

Almond Flour Bread

2 cups finely ground almonds (best if ground until it becomes nut butter)
3 organic egg whites
1 tablespoon organic coconut oil, liquified
½ teaspoon soda
¼ teaspoon salt

Preheat oven to 350 degrees F.

Whip egg whites until soft peaks. In food processor or blender grind almonds, soda and salt, add in coconut oil. Fold ground mixture into whipped egg whites.

Place into a greased bread pan and bake until light brown on top and a toothpick comes out clean from the center of the loaf.

E-Z Tortillas

1¼ cup of buckwheat or millet flour
¼ teaspoon salt
½ cup water, room temperature
½–1 teaspoon safflower oil, optional—but use it especially with millet

Preheat a large griddle or skillet.

Whisk 1 cup of flour and the salt together in a bowl. Make a well in the center and pour in the oil and water. Stir with a fork until the dough clumps together in a ball.

Scatter the remaining ¼ cup of flour on a board or piece of wax or parchment paper. Make golfball size balls of dough and roll them in flour. Flatten with your hand, turning often to keep them floured. As the dough absorbs flour, the texture becomes more workable.

Roll each tortilla thinner with a rolling pin. When thin, and approx 6 inches bake them on the hot griddle. Use no oil. Bake about 3 minutes on each side. Put the baked tortillas on wire racks or lay them on cotton towels.

Buckwheat Banana Bread

2 tablespoons organic flax seeds, ground
⅓ cup water
1⅓ cups buckwheat groats, unroasted
½ cup organic pumpkin seeds
2 tablespoons tapioca starch flour
½ teaspoon nutmeg or cinnamon, optional
⅔ cup chopped walnuts, optional
¼ cup organic walnut oil
2 cups mashed bananas, approximately 4 medium
2 teaspoons non-aluminum baking soda
2 tablespoons boiling water

Preheat oven to 400. Oil and flour an 8x4 inch loaf pan.

Combine flax seeds with water in a small saucepan. Bring to a rolling boil and immediately remove from heat. Set aside to soak until needed.

In a blender, grind ⅓ cup of the groats into fine flour. Push through a strainer over a mixing bowl and return pieces to blender: Repeat until all have been ground.

Combine pumpkin seeds, tapioca starch, salt and spices. Blend on high 1 minute, stopping to scrape bottom. Add seed mixture and nuts directly into the flour; and whisk together well.

Measure 2¼ cups of water; pour into the blender jar, mark the level and discard the water. Place oil and 1 cup bananas, broken into 1" chunks into blender and mix. Continue to add banana chunks until the 2¼ cup level is reached.

Pour the liquid mixture over dry ingredients and mix thoroughly. Dissolve baking soda in boiling water. Add to the batter and stir swiftly until water disappears, do not beat it.

Quickly scrape batter into pan and place in hot oven and immediately reduce temperature to 325 degrees F.

Bake for 70 minutes or until a toothpick in middle comes out dry. Remove from the oven and cool in the pan for 10 minutes. Turn out on a wire rack and cool completely before slicing.

Flax Crackers

4 cups whole organic flax seeds
⅓ to ½ cup Braggs amino acids
2–3 lemons, juiced
4 teaspoons organic butter
½ teaspoon non-aluminum baking powder
½ cup organic coconut milk (just coconut milk and guar gum)

Preheat oven to 325 degrees F.

Soak flax seeds 4–6 hours, which will make a gelatinous mixture.

Add Braggs, butter, baking powder and lemon juice to taste and mix well until dough forms. Wrap in parchment or wax paper and chill for 10 minutes.

Turn out on a floured board, parchment or wax paper and cut into quarters. Roll and spread each quarter as thin as possible, 1/16th of an inch. Cut into squares about 2 to 2½ inches and place on an ungreased baking sheet.

Bake 20 minutes or until crisp.

Options: You can add garlic, onions, various herbs and seasonings, or sun-dried tomatoes to make different flavors and tastes.

Buckwheat Crackers

1 cup buckwheat flour
¼ cup arrowroot powder
3 tablespoons organic sesame seeds
2 tablespoons organic cold pressed sesame oil
½ cup water

Preheat oven to 400. Oil the center of a cookie sheet; leave the outer 1" from edge unoiled.

Mix the flour, arrowroot and seeds in a small bowl. Make a hole in the center, pour in the oil and water, stir with a fork until dough clumps and forms a ball. Scrape the ball of dough onto the middle of the cookie sheet. Pat it into a flat rectangle.

Oil one side of a sheet of wax or parchment paper. Place the oiled side down on the dough. Roll the dough out very thin. Cut into 2-inch squares.

Place in the oven and reduce oven temperature to 350 degrees F. Remove after 12 minutes and lift off the crispy crackers around the outer edge. Place on a wire rack to cool.

Separate the remaining crackers. Turn the oven off and return those crackers to the oven for 10–20 minutes until they are crisp.

Flat Bread

1 cup chickpea flour
1 cup pounded organic yam flour
1 tablespoon safflower oil
Water

Mix the two flours together with water and oil, a little at a time, to produce a dough. Leave the dough in the refrigerator to rest for 1 hour. Make small balls and flatten, then cook in a flat skillet or on a griddle with no oil.

The dough can be refrigerated for a few days. The cooked flat bread can be frozen and reheated in the toaster.

CAKES AND COOKIES

cake: a sweet baked food made from a dough or thick batter

cook·ie: a small flat or slightly raised cake

Cakes and Cookies

Meringue Cookies

3 large organic egg whites
¼ teaspoon cream of tartar
1 tablespoon plus 1½ teaspoon of stevia crushed leaf powder
1 teaspoon non-alcohol vanilla extract

Preheat oven to 250 degrees F. Place racks in upper and lower third of oven. Line two baking sheets with parchment paper or a Silpat liner. You can form the cookies with a pastry bag fitted with a ½ inch tip, plain or star, or with two spoons.

In the bowl of electric mixer fitted with whisk attachment, beat the egg whites on low-medium speed until foamy. Add the cream of tartar and continue to beat the whites until they hold soft peaks. Add the stevia and beat until the meringue holds very stiff peaks. Beat in the vanilla extract.

Onto the prepared cookie sheets pipe or spoon 2-inch rounds of meringue mixture in rows about ½ inch apart. Bake for approximately one hour, rotating the baking sheets from top to bottom and front to back about half way through to ensure even baking. The meringue is done cooking when pale ivory in color and firm enough to lift from the sheet without sticking.

Test by removing one and letting it cool for a few minutes. When broken in half it should be crisp and dry. When cooked, turn off the oven, open the door and leave cookies in oven to dry for a few hours.

Makes 3 to 4 dozen

Variation: Almond Meringue Cookies, add in 1½ cups finely ground almonds along with vanilla.

Almond Cake

1 cup organic butter, softened
1 tablespoon crushed stevia leaf powder

5 organic eggs
2 cups ground almond flour
1 teaspoon non-aluminum baking powder
1 tablespoon lemon juice
1 teaspoon non-alcohol vanilla extract
1 teaspoon non-alcohol almond extract (optional)

Preheat the oven to 350 degrees F. Butter and line two 8-inch round baking pans with parchment paper.

In a food processor, mix the butter, stevia, eggs, almond flour, baking powder, lemon juice, vanilla and almond extract together until smooth.

Divide the mixture between the two baking pans, level the tops by banging the pan on counter once. Bake for 30 minutes until firm in the center.

Remove from oven and place on cooling rack for 5 minutes. Loosen edges with a knife and turn out onto a rack. Peel off the paper and cool completely.

When cool turn one cake upside down and spread with coconut cream (see condiments), top with other cake and frost with more coconut cream.

Serves 10

Almond Flour Pound Cake

1 cup organic butter
1 tablespoon crushed stevia leaf powder
5 organic eggs
2 cups almond flour
1 teaspoon non-aluminum baking powder
1 teaspoon lemon extract
1 teaspoon non alcohol vanilla extract

Preheat oven to 350 degrees F. Grease a 9-inch cake pan.

Mix butter and stevia well; add eggs, one at a time, beating after each.

Mix flour with baking powder and add to egg mixture a little at a time while beating. Add lemon and vanilla extract. Blend well.

Pour into greased pan and bake for 50–55 minutes. Cool in pan for 5 minutes, loosen sides and turn out onto a rack to cool completely.

Carrot Cake

4 organic eggs
2 organic egg yolks
2 tablespoons crushed stevia leaf powder
1¼ cups almond flour
1 cup finely grated carrots
2 sticks butter, melted
Juice and zest from 2 lemons

Pre-heat oven to 350 degrees F. Grease and flour a loaf pan.

Melt butter and set aside to cool.

In a medium bowl beat eggs with 2 additional yolks and add stevia. Add almond flour and mix until well combined. Add in lemon juice and zest, fold in grated carrots and stir in melted butter.

Bake for approximately 35 minutes. Remove pan to a wire rack and cool for 10–15 minutes. Remove from pan and cool completely.

Macaroons

2⅔ cups shredded organic unsweetened coconut
1 cup sliced raw almonds
1½ teaspoon crushed stevia leaf powder
4 large organic egg whites

Preheat oven to 325 degrees F. Grease 2 large cookie sheets.

Into a large bowl, add coconut, almonds, and stevia. Mix until combined. Stir in egg whites until well blended.

Drop by heaping tablespoons, about 2 inches apart, on cookie sheets, place sheets on 2 oven racks. Bake 20 to 25 minutes until golden, rotating cookie sheets between upper and lower racks halfway through baking time.

With a flat spatula or pancake turner, remove cookies to wire racks to cool completely. Store cookies in tightly covered container.

Almond Macaroons

1¼ cup almonds
⅛ teaspoon cinnamon
2 tablespoons grated lemon peel
2 egg whites, beaten
1½ teaspoon crushed stevia leaf powder
2 tablespoons lemon juice

Preheat oven to 250 degrees F.

Grind almonds coarsely, add cinnamon, lemon peel and set aside. Beat egg whites until very stiff. Add in stevia and continue beating. Fold into the egg whites the almond mixture and lemon juice and blend.

Drop teaspoonfuls onto a baking sheet lined with parchment paper or a Silpat sheet. Bake 20 minutes.

Remove from baking sheet with a flat spatula or pancake turner while still slightly warm.

Makes 30 macaroons

Flourless Chocolate Cake

4 organic eggs, separated
¾ cup butter
2 tablespoons crushed stevia leaf powder
1½ pounds 100% cocoa unsweetened baking chocolate, melted and cooled slightly
2½ cups coconut whipped cream (see condiments)

Preheat oven to 350 degrees F. Grease and line with parchment paper a 10-inch cake pan that is at least 2 inches deep. Set aside.

Break chocolate in pieces and melt over hot water in a double boiler. Set aside to cool.

Beat egg yolks and add stevia. Gently fold in melted butter and cooled chocolate. Beat egg whites until frothy and stiff peaks form. Fold into chocolate mixture.

Pour mixture into prepared pan and set pan into center of oven.

Bake 40 minutes or until toothpick inserted into center comes out clean and cake pulls away from sides of pan.

Remove from oven and cool completely. Center of cake will fall slightly after it cools. Refrigerate about 30 minutes, then invert onto a serving platter and glaze.

Glaze:

2 squares 100% cocoa unsweetened chocolate
½ stick butter, softened
¾ teaspoon crushed stevia leaf powder

Melt chocolate in a double boiler.

Stir in butter and stevia, stirring constantly and cook over low heat until thickened. Spread over cooled cake with a rubber spatula.

Serves 12

Flourless Carrot Cake

1 cup almonds, with skins
2 large carrots, peeled and trimmed
Finely grated zest of ½ lemon
Juice of ½ lemon
1 teaspoon non-alcohol vanilla
1 tablespoon plus 1½ teaspoon crushed stevia leaf powder
3 large organic eggs, separated

4 tablespoons cornstarch
½ teaspoon non-aluminum baking powder
1 tablespoon pine nuts

Preheat oven to 350F. Butter the sides of an 8x2-inch cake pan, line the base with a circle of parchment and butter the parchment.

Grind almonds to flour and set aside. Grate carrots into fine shreds. There should be 1½ cups, quite firmly packed. Place in a bowl, add lemon zest, lemon juice and set aside.

Beat egg whites until they start to stiffen, add stevia and continue beating until stiff and glossy.

Beat egg yolks until very thick and pale lemon in color. Stir in carrot mixture, ground almonds and fold in egg whites. Sift cornstarch and baking powder on top and fold in lightly but thoroughly.

Spoon into prepared pan, smooth top with a rubber spatula, and sprinkle with pine nuts. Bake for 40 minutes, until a tester comes out dry. Let cool in pan for 10 minutes.

Run a knife blade around edge of cake and unmold onto a rack. Peel off paper, reverse onto rack right side up, and let cool completely.

S Cookies

1 cup organic butter, softened
1 teaspoon non-alcohol vanilla extract
1 tablespoon crushed stevia leaf powder
2 organic egg yolks
2½ cups almond flour

Preheat oven to 350 degrees F.

Combine butter and vanilla until soft and add stevia. Beat in egg yolks one at a time; add flour slowly blending well after each addition.

Fill a cookie press about ⅔ full and press out cookies in "S" shapes on greased and lightly floured baking sheets. If you do not have a press, you can also spoon teaspoonfuls onto baking sheet.

Bake 12 to 14 minutes, or until golden yellow on edges. Watch the cookies while they bake because they burn easily

Makes 6 dozen

Almond Cookies

Note: Spelt is wheat; celiac sufferers should not use this recipe. Candida should only eat in rotation when on maintenance.

1 cup organic almond butter (or sesame tahini)
1 tablespoon plus 1½ teaspoon crushed stevia leaf powder
1 teaspoon non-alcohol vanilla extract
¼ cup organic sunflower or safflower oil
1 cup spelt flour
1 cup quinoa flour
9 whole almonds cut in half

Preheat oven to 375 F.

In a small bowl blend almond butter, stevia, oil and vanilla. Sift together flours and combine with almond butter mixture. Using your hands form into small balls and place on an oiled cookie sheet.

Press each cookie with the tines of a fork. Cut almonds in half and press one, cut side up, into each cookie.

Bake for 12–15 minutes or just until browned.

Makes 1½ dozen

CHILI, SOUPS AND STEWS

chili: a thick sauce of meat and chilies

soup: a liquid food especially with a meat, fish or vegetable stock as a base and often containing pieces of solid food

stew: fish or meat usually with vegetables prepared by simmering or slow boiling

Chili, Soups, and Stews

Chicken Wild Rice Soup

½ cup butter
1 onion, finely chopped
½ cup celery, chopped
½ cup carrots, sliced
6 cups chicken broth
2 cups cooked wild rice
1 pound boneless skinless chicken breasts, cooked and cubed
½ teaspoon curry powder
½ teaspoon mustard powder
½ teaspoon dried parsley
½ teaspoon ground black pepper
1 cup slivered almonds
2 cups coconut milk

Melt butter in a large saucepan over medium heat. Stir in the onion, celery and carrots and sauté for 5 minutes.

Gradually pour in the chicken broth, stirring constantly, until all added. Bring just to a boil, reduce heat to low and let simmer.

Add the rice, chicken, curry powder, mustard, parsley, and pepper. Let simmer for 1 to 2 hours.

Pour in the coconut milk and add almonds, allow to heat through, approximately 1 minute.

Serves 4 to 6

Vegetable Beef Soup

8 ounces lean beef, round or rump
5 cups beef stock
1 large carrot, diced

2 celery stalks, diced
1 medium onion, chopped
1 leek
¼ teaspoon basil
¼ teaspoon marjoram
⅛ teaspoon oregano
Pepper to taste
2 tablespoons parsley, chopped

With stock in a saucepan add the basil, marjoram and oregano, and bring to a boil.

Clean the leek by cutting in to 3 inch pieces and separate all the pieces from each other, place in a large bowl of water to soak. This removes any additional hidden dirt.

Cut the meat into thin strips and add to the stock along with the carrots, onion and celery. Remove leeks from water, dry and cut into thin strips and add to stock.

Bring back to a boil, reduce heat, cover and simmer approximately 20 minutes until the meat and vegetables are tender.

Skim any film at the top of the liquid and blot the surface with paper towel to remove fat. Add pepper to taste.

Serves 4

Wild Rice Turkey Chili

1 tablespoon olive oil
1 tablespoon butter
1 medium onion, chopped
2 cloves garlic, minced
3 cups cooked turkey, cubed
2 cups cooked wild rice
1 15-ounce can white beans
2 cans diced chilies
15 ounces chicken broth
1 teaspoon cumin powder

Sauté the onion and garlic in the butter and olive oil until soft. Add the remaining ingredients and heat through.

Serves 4

Buckwheat Vegetable Soup

1 tablespoon extra virgin or cold pressed olive oil
1 medium leek
2 rutabagas
2 carrots
½ cup buckwheat groats
4 cups vegetable broth
Freshly ground pepper

Wash leeks, thoroughly and slice thinly discarding the last 2 inches of the green tops. Place in a bowl of water to soak out any remaining grit.

Wash and peel the rutabagas and carrots and cut into small cubes about 1 inch. Heat the olive oil over medium heat in a large pot. Add vegetables and fry for about 2 minutes, stirring constantly. Add groats and vegetable broth.

Bring to a boil and then turn heat to low. Simmer for about 30 minutes. Season to taste with pepper.

Serves 4–6

Hot Soba Noodle Soup

4 pieces of tofu, cut into large triangles
1 package of soba noodles
4 green onions, finely slivered on the diagonal
6½ cups of dashi (see below)
3 tablespoons of Bragg's amino acids
⅜ tablespoon of crushed stevia leaf powder

In a skillet with approximately 1 inch of coconut oil, fry tofu. Drain. In a saucepan, simmer the tofu in one cup of dashi.

Meanwhile cook the soba noodles and rinse using hot water, drain, and then transfer to serving bowl, place the tofu on top. Add Braggs and stevia to the dashi, pour the hot broth over the noodles and garnish with the green onions.

Making Dashi:

Place two quarts of cold water in a large deep pot. Take 1½-ounces, approximately 20 inches, of konbu/kelp and carefully wipe with a clean moistened cloth. Do not wash as it removes the flavor. Place the konbu into the pot and slowly bring the water to just before boiling, regulate the heat so that the water never actually boils. Once the kelp is tender, approximately 15 minutes, remove the seaweed.

Add 3 cups of loose bonito flakes and turn off the heat. Once the flakes have sunk to the bottom of the pot—approximately 1–2 minutes—strain stock into another pot using a colander filled with cheesecloth or a large coffee filter.

The finished dashi should be a light golden color and free of any flakes. You can store it in the refrigerator for up to three days but best to use as soon as made.

Fish Soup

1 pound of firm white fish filets (cod, or halibut) cut in 1-inch pieces
1 tablespoon extra virgin or cold pressed olive oil
1 large onion, chopped
2 cloves garlic, diced
1¾ cups fish stock
⅓ cup lemon juice
1 bay leaf
1 sprig each of fresh thyme, rosemary and oregano
1 pound mussels, cleaned
8 ounces shrimp, peeled and cleaned
1½ cups of chopped tomatoes
Pepper to taste

Heat a skillet with oil and sauté the onion and garlic for 3 minutes, just until soft. Add the stock and bring to a boil, reduce heat to a simmer. Add in the lemon juice.

Tie together with a piece of kitchen string sprig of thyme, rosemary and oregano and add to pan with the fish filets and mussels. Cover and simmer for 5 minutes. Discard any mussels that do not open.

Add the tomatoes and shrimp and cook another 3 minutes until shrimp is pink and cooked through. Do not overcook the shrimp, it will rubberize, season with pepper to taste. Remove the herbs before serving.

Serves 4

Chicken and Beans Chili

1 to 1½ pound chicken tenderloins, cut in ½ inch pieces
1 cup chopped onion
1 15-ounce can beans—pinto, white, or small red, drained
1 15-ounce can black beans, drained
2 pounds tomatoes, peeled, cut into pieces
⅛ teaspoon pepper
¼ teaspoon crushed stevia leaf powder
1 tablespoon coconut oil
1 tablespoon butter
1 tablespoon finely minced onion
1 tablespoon finely minced green bell pepper
¼ teaspoon cumin
¼ teaspoon chili powder
¼ teaspoon garlic powder

In large skillet with oil, brown chicken and onion over medium heat.

Stir in beans, chili powder, tomatoes, pepper, mix in stevia, butter, onion, bell pepper, and cumin, with chili and garlic powder; bring to a boil. Reduce to low; simmer for about 20 minutes.

Serves 6

Cold Cucumber Soup

1 medium cucumber, peeled and seeded
1⅔ cup vegetable stock, cold
⅔ cup tomato juice
1⅔ cup plain unsweetened yogurt
1 tablespoon mint, chopped
White pepper

Dice the cucumber before putting in a blender or food processor and blend to a puree. Place in a bowl with fish stock and tomato juice, yogurt and mix well. Add pepper to taste. Stir in chopped mint, cover and chill for at least 2 hours.

Variation: You can add in 4 ½ ounces of chopped shrimp or crabmeat.

Serves 4

Beef Stew

1½ pounds beef stew meat, cut into 1-inch cubes
2 tablespoons extra virgin or cold pressed olive oil
½ cup onion, chopped
1 clove garlic, minced
½ teaspoon dried thyme, crushed
2 cups vegetable juice
1 teaspoon instant beef bouillon granules
2 medium turnips, peeled and cubed into 1 inch pieces
1½ cup sliced celery
1½ cups sliced carrot
Few dashes of hot pepper sauce

In large saucepan brown meat in hot oil a few pieces at a time. Return all meat to pan and add onion, garlic and thyme.

Stir in vegetable juice, bouillon, hot pepper sauce and 1 cup of water. Bring to a boil, then reduce heat, cover and simmer 1 ¼-hours until meat is tender.

Stir in celery and carrot, cover and simmer for 30 minutes more.

Serves 6

Chicken Leek Soup

12 ounces boneless chicken
¾ cup leeks cut in 1-inch pieces
5 cups chicken stock
2 tablespoons butter
3 stalks parsley
1 sprig thyme
1 bay leaf
White pepper

Cut leeks in to 1 inch pieces, separate the layers and place in a large bowl of water, and soak to remove any dirt.

Cut the chicken in to 1-inch pieces.

In a large saucepan, melt the butter and add the chicken and leeks. Stir and cook approximately 8 minutes, stirring occasionally.

Add chicken stock. Tie kitchen string around the parsley, thyme and bay leaf. And add to the pot.

Bring to a boil, reduce heat and simmer over low heat for 45 minutes. Add pepper to taste. Remove herb package before serving.

Serves 6

Lentil Soup

2⅓ cups dry lentils
8 cups water
1 16-ounce can tomatoes, cut up
2 slices pancetta, cut up
½ cup onion, chopped

½ cup carrot, chopped
3 tablespoons parsley
2 tablespoons lemon juice
1 clove garlic, minced
½ teaspoon dried oregano, crushed
¼ teaspoon freshly ground pepper

Clean and soak lentils and put in a large saucepan with water, bring to a boil and add tomatoes, pancetta, onion, carrot, parsley, lemon juice, garlic, oregano and pepper.

Bring back to a boil, reduce heat, cover and simmer 45 minutes.

Serves 8 to 10

Pork Soup

1½-pounds boneless pork, cut into ½ inch cubes
2 tablespoons extra virgin or cold pressed olive oil
½ cup finely chopped onion
2 cloves garlic, minced
1 teaspoon paprika
4 cups water
1 tablespoon beef bouillon granules
2 medium carrots cut into ½ inch pieces
1 pound winter squash, cut into 1-inch cubes
1 medium tomato, peeled and chopped
¼ teaspoon ground red pepper
2 cups torn fresh spinach

In a large skillet or Dutch oven heat oil and cook half the meat until well browned. Set aside. Put the other half of the meat in pan with onion, garlic, and paprika and cook until browned. Return other portion of meat to pan and stir in water and beef bouillon granules. Bring to a boil, reduce heat to simmer, cover and cook for 1 hour.

Add carrots, squash, tomato and red pepper. Cover and simmer another 15 to 20 minutes until vegetables are tender. Stir in spinach and simmer 3 to 5 minutes more.

Serves 8

Minestrone Soup

1½-cups dry navy beans
9 cups water
1 cup carrots, chopped
6 slices pancetta, cooked crisp
2 tablespoons bacon drippings
1 cup onion, chopped
1 clove garlic, minced
1 16-ounce can tomato, cut up with juice
2 cups finely shredded cabbage
1 17-ounce can peas, drained
1 medium zucchini, sliced
1 teaspoon dried basil
½ teaspoon dried sage

Rinse beans and put in a large saucepan with 9 cups of water. Bring to boil and reduce to simmer and cook for 2 minutes. Remove from heat, cover and let stand 1 hour. Do not drain.

Add carrots cover and simmer 2 ½ to 3 hours.

In a large skillet with the pancetta drippings cook onion, celery and garlic with tomatoes and liquid, cabbage, zucchini, peas, basil, sage and ¼ teaspoon pepper.

Add to saucepan, bring to a boil, reduce heat and simmer 25 minutes. Stir in pancetta before serving.

Serves 8

CONDIMENTS AND SPREADS

con·di·ment: something used to enhance the flavor of food

spread: to apply on a surface, a food to be spread

Condiments and Spreads

Chili Sauce

2 cups canned organic tomatoes
1 onion, chopped
Dash of cayenne pepper
⅛ teaspoon cloves
⅛ teaspoon cinnamon
⅜ tablespoon crushed stevia leaf powder
¼ cup lemon juice
2 tablespoons chopped green pepper

In a heavy-bottomed saucepan, combine the tomatoes, onion, cayenne, cloves, cinnamon, stevia, and lemon juice.

Simmer, uncovered, for 1 hour. Add the green pepper and simmer 30 minutes more. Add salt to taste, if needed. Chill before serving.

Makes 1½ cups

Carrot Almond Butter Spread

4 cups thinly sliced carrots (about 1 pound)
1 cup water
¼ cup almond butter (store bought or see condiments)
1 tablespoon Bragg's amino acids

Pressure-cook or boil carrots in water until soft. Drain and reserve broth.

Puree carrots in a blender with remaining ingredients. Gradually add broth only if needed for a creamier texture.

French Onion Spread

1 tablespoon extra virgin or cold pressed olive oil
2 yellow onions, sliced thin
2 cloves garlic, sliced thin
Pinch of freshly ground black pepper
1 tablespoon dried rosemary
1 tablespoon dried basil
1 tablespoon dried oregano
2 teaspoons dried sage
2 teaspoons thyme
2 teaspoons marjoram
1 tablespoon sesame tahini
1 tablespoon chives
8 ounces fresh feta cheese

Heat oil in a frying pan and add onions and garlic sauté briefly. Stir in pepper and spices. Cover and cook 10 to 15 minutes until onions are soft and lightly browned. Pour off any liquid. Cool slightly.

Place cooled mixture in a food processor or blender and puree with feta cheese.

Lemon Butter

3 organic eggs, beaten just to mix
2 tablespoons organic butter
6 tablespoons water
3 tablespoons crushed stevia leaf powder
¼ teaspoon grated lemon rind
2 lemons, thoroughly juiced

Place egg yolks, lemon juice, and stevia in top of a double boiler, add the butter.

Beat whites of the eggs until slightly stiff and add to double boiler.

Cook on double boiler stirring well until thickened. Add the rind, take off heat, pour into a dish, and chill.

Tartar Sauce

1 cup mayonnaise (see condiments)
¼ cup finely chopped onion
1 tablespoon lemon juice
½ teaspoon dried dill

Mix all ingredients well. Chill for one hour for best flavor.

Makes approximately 1¼ cup

Hollandaise Sauce

2 organic eggs
2 tablespoons lemon juice
Few red pepper flakes
⅓ cup organic butter

Combine eggs, lemon juice and pepper flakes in a blender, mix.

Turn the setting to medium speed and add the hot butter a little at a time until incorporated. Remove from blender. Serve immediately.

Makes 1 cup

Coconut Sour Cream

1 cup chilled coconut milk (just coconut milk and guar gum)
2–4 drops of lemon juice

Thoroughly chill coconut milk. Place in a food processor or a non-reactive bowl.

Add one drop of lemon juice and blend then taste. Continue adding one drop of lemon juice at time blending after each drop and tasting until to your taste.

Pico de Gallo Salsa

3 fresh jalapenos, stemmed, seeded and finely chopped
4–5 fresh red tomatoes, diced
½ bunch fresh cilantro, coarsely chopped; approx. 3 tablespoons
1 small onion, diced
2 tablespoons lime juice
3 cloves garlic, minced

Combine all ingredients and marinate for at least one hour to allow natural juices to combine. Chill well before serving. Garnish with wedge of lime.

Coconut Whipped Cream

1 can coconut milk (just coconut milk and guar gum)
2 teaspoons of non-alcohol vanilla and a piece of vanilla bean
Dash of nutmeg
Dash of cinnamon
Stevia to your taste
2 tablespoons cornstarch

Combine 2 tablespoons of cornstarch with equal amount of coconut milk. In a saucepan, combine remaining coconut milk with vanilla, nutmeg, and cinnamon. Add stevia to sweetness of choice. Add in cornstarch mixture and cook over medium heat until thickened to a consistency of a pudding.

Cool and serve.

Tomato Catsup

2 cups tomato paste
½ cup lemon juice
½ cup water
1 teaspoon oregano
⅛ teaspoon cumin
⅛ teaspoon nutmeg
⅛ teaspoon pepper

½ teaspoon dry mustard
Dash garlic powder

Mix all ingredients in a food processor and blend well.

Makes approximately 2½ cups

Mayonnaise

1 organic egg
½ teaspoon dry mustard
1 cup extra virgin or cold pressed olive oil
1 ½ tablespoons lemon juice
1 tablespoon boiling water

Place the egg, mustard and ¼ cup of the oil in an electric blender. While blending, add the remaining ¾ cup oil in a slow, thin stream. Add lemon juice and water. Refrigerate.

Note: if using a food processor, add an extra egg yolk, omit the water, and use up to ½ cup more oil, and adjust lemon juice to taste.

Makes 1½ cups

Aioli (Garlic Mayonnaise)

5 large garlic cloves, peeled
2 organic egg yolks, lightly beaten
2 cups extra virgin or cold pressed olive oil
Juice of 1 lemon

Pound the garlic cloves to make a paste.

In a bowl with the egg yolks add garlic and mix with a wooden spoon in one direction. Slowly add the oil, one drop at a time, until approximately 4 tablespoons of the oil are mixed and the eggs start to pale in color. The mixture should be thick.

Add approximately 1 tablespoon of water and 1 teaspoon of lemon juice and continue stirring, add more oil in a thin stream. When thick again add 1 more tablespoon of water and 1 teaspoon lemon juice. Repeat until all oil is used.

If the mayonnaise breaks: Place into a clean bowl, add in a garlic clove, 1 tablespoon lukewarm water and 1 egg yolk, crush and mix together stirring constantly in one direction.

Makes approx 2½ cups

Black Olive Pesto

½ cup black olives, pitted and chopped
2 cloves of garlic, mashed
1 teaspoon basil
1 shallot, quartered
1 teaspoon tarragon
2 tablespoons lemon juice
½ cup extra virgin or cold pressed olive oil
½ cup sun-dried tomatoes, oil packed

Put olives, garlic, basil, shallot, tarragon, lemon juice and tomatoes in a food processor and blend, drizzle in olive oil and continue to blend until a paste.

Makes 2 cups

Horseradish Sauce

¼ teaspoon crushed stevia leaf powder
¾ cup plain unsweetened yogurt, drained
¾ cup mayonnaise (see condiments)
3 tablespoons lemon juice
1 tablespoon mustard, made from dry mustard powder and water
3 tablespoons grated fresh organic horseradish
½ teaspoon ground red pepper

Combine in a small non-reactive bowl the mustard powder and water, mix well, add in remaining ingredients and blend with a whisk. Cover and chill thoroughly.

Roasted Garlic Guacamole Dip

4 garlic cloves, unpeeled
Olive oil
2 avocados, peeled and pitted
1 tablespoon lime juice or more to taste
Freshly ground black pepper to taste

Preheat the oven to 350°F.

Place the unpeeled garlic cloves in the center of a large square of aluminum foil. Drizzle with olive oil. Wrap the foil around the cloves and pinch the edges to seal. Place the foil packet in the oven and let bake for 45 minutes or until the garlic is very tender. Remove from the oven and let cool briefly. Peel off the outer skins. Note: this step can be done the day before.

In a medium bowl, mash the avocado with the roasted garlic. Stir in lime juice and season to taste with freshly ground black pepper.

Makes 1 cup

Citrus Salsa

2 navel oranges
¼ cup finely diced red onion
¼ cup coarsely chopped cilantro
½ hot red chili pepper, seeded, stemmed and minced
1 tablespoon fresh lime juice
Salt and freshly ground black pepper to taste

Peel the oranges, removing all the bitter white pith. Working over a bowl, cut between the membranes to release the orange segments. Squeeze the orange after removing membranes to extract the remaining juice.

Stir in the red onion, cilantro, chili pepper and the lime juice. Adjust seasonings to taste with pepper and more lime juice if needed.

Makes 1 cup

Almond Milk

1 cup organic almonds
4 cups water

Start with whole almonds and soak overnight in water. Next day, blanch almonds by placing into a stainless steel strainer and dip into boiling water. Remove the skins; they come right off.

Puree in blender with water. Filter out the grit by straining through cheesecloth lining a strainer. You may need to squeeze the cheesecloth.

Variation: add stevia and vanilla for sweeter milk for use in desserts and pastries

Green Chili Salsa

3 pounds green chilies
1 small yellow onion
2 medium tomatoes
6 sprigs fresh cilantro
1 small lemon

Wash chilies and roast whole under broiler until skin blackens, turning to roast all sides. Place in a bowl of ice water for 5 minutes. Carefully peel blackened skins from chilies and discard. Cut open, clean and discard stems and seeds. Coarsely chop.

Thoroughly wash your hands after handling chilies and never touch your eyes.

Finely dice onion, quarter and seed tomatoes then chop. Remove stems from the cilantro leaves and finely chop. Mix chopped chilies, onions, tomatoes, and cilantro. Squeeze the juice of the lemon over the mixture. Stir.

If you want a spicier salsa, add a few red pepper flakes.

Makes 3 cups

Tahini

2 tablespoons sesame seeds
½ teaspoon sesame oil
¼ teaspoon salt
¼ cup tepid water

Blend sesame seeds in a blender and grind until smooth. Add sesame oil and slowly add ¼ cup of water while blending. Blend until completely smooth.

Makes ½ cup

Almond Nut Butter

2 cups raw almonds
1–2 tablespoons safflower oil, optional

Blanch almonds in boiling water by plunging almonds in a stainless steel strainer into the water for 30 seconds; set aside for 3 minutes to cool.

Remove skins from cooled almonds and pat dry. In a skillet cook over medium heat 3–4 minutes or until lightly toasted and fragrant. Remove from the heat and allow the almonds to cool.

Transfer the cooled almonds to a blender or food processor and process for 1–2 minutes to finely grind them to a powder. Scrape down the sides of the container. Continue to process the almonds an additional 1–2 minutes, adding some safflower oil to form a smooth and creamy paste.

Transfer the almond butter to an airtight container and store in the refrigerator.

Makes 1 cup

Poultry Seasoning

¾ teaspoon sage, crumbled
¼ teaspoon thyme, crumbled
¼ teaspoon pepper

Dash marjoram
Dash cloves, optional

Store in a tightly closed jar.

DESSERTS

des·sert: a usually sweet course or dish (as of pastry or ice cream) served at the end of a meal

Desserts

Almond Chocolate Chip Biscotti

Note: Spelt is wheat; celiac sufferers should not use this recipe. Candida should only eat in rotation when on maintenance.

3 cups spelt flour
3 teaspoons non-aluminum baking powder
½ cup butter, room temperature
1 tablespoon crushed stevia leaf powder
3 large organic eggs, 1 egg white separated
¼ teaspoon non-alcohol almond extract
½ teaspoon cinnamon
½ cup slivered almonds
¾ cup chocolate chunks of 100% cocoa unsweetened chocolate
Zest of one medium large lemon (optional)

Preheat oven to 350 degrees F. Grease a cookie sheet.

Combine into a medium bowl flour, baking powder, stevia and cinnamon. Add almonds and cut in butter using fingers or two butter knives until well blended.

Make a well in flour mix and add the eggs, zest, chocolate and almond extract and mix until a smooth ball. Dough should be firm but manageable, if too sticky add more flour.

Roll dough into an oblong ½ inch thick and place on cookie sheet and brush top with reserved egg white. Bake in oven for 30 minutes until golden brown.

Cool for 10 minutes and then cut into ¾ inch thick pieces.

Makes approximately 12

Pastry

2½ cups almond flour
⅔ cup coconut oil
¼ teaspoon salt
⅓ cup water

Preheat oven to 450 degrees F.

Combine flour and salt in a mixing bowl. Cut shortening into flour with a pastry blender or two butter knives, do not over mix; it should resemble peas.

Add water gradually, sprinkling a little at a time over the mixture. Use only enough water to hold the pastry together when pressed between the fingers, it should not feel wet.

Roll dough into a round ball, handling as little as possible. Roll out on a lightly floured board into a circle ⅛ in thick and one inch larger than the diameter of the top of the pie pan and trim to the edge of the pie pan. Prick with a fork. Bake for 12–15 minutes or until a golden brown.

Fluffy, Flaky Pastry Sheet

4 organic eggs, separated
¼ teaspoon cream of tartar
1 teaspoon of non-alcohol vanilla extract
⅜ teaspoon crushed stevia leaf powder

Beat egg whites with cream of tartar until stiff peaks form. Set aside.

Combine egg yolk, vanilla, and stevia and mix well. Fold gently into egg white mixture.

Spread on a baking sheet and smooth. Bake for 20 minutes until puffed and brown. Cut into desired sized pieces.

Almond Cinnamon Pie Crust

¼ cup almond flour
¾ cup soy flour
½ cup arrowroot powder
¼ teaspoon salt
½ teaspoon cinnamon
3 tablespoons vegetable oil
3–4 tablespoons ice water

Preheat oven to 400°F. Oil a 9 inch pie plate.

Combine flours, arrowroot, salt, and cinnamon; blend well.

Combine oil and 3 tablespoons of water, and blend with fork. Add all at once to flour mixture. Stir only until a ball forms. If dry and crumbly add a little more water, one teaspoon at a time, until ball hangs together.

Pat or roll crust to fit pie plate. Dough tears easily, but mends using extra bits to patch.

Prick with fork. Bake for 18 minutes until crisp. Cool and fill.

Chocolate Ricotta Pie

Note: opinion as to the allowed use of cream cheese is divided—decide for yourself or consult your practitioner

1½ cups almond flour
2 tablespoons cornstarch
¾ cup raw pine nuts, plus ¾ cup, toasted (about 8 ounces in total)
2 tablespoons crushed stevia leaf powder
1 stick (4 ounces) unsalted butter, melted and cooled slightly
½ cup water
8 ounces 100% cocoa unsweetened chocolate cut in chips; approximately 1⅓ cups
¾ cup ricotta cheese
3 ounces organic cream cheese made with vegetable rennet, at room temperature

1 large organic egg
3 large organic egg yolks

Blend the flour, cornstarch, ¾ cup pine nuts and 1½ teaspoons of stevia in a food processor until finely ground. Add the butter and pulse, just until dough forms.

Press the dough over the bottom and 2 inches up the sides of an 11-inch diameter tart pan with a removable bottom. Refrigerate until the dough is firm, about 30 minutes.

Preheat oven to 350 degrees F.

Line the tart dough with aluminum foil and fill with pie weights or dried beans. Bake the in the lower third of the oven until just set, approximately 25 minutes. Carefully remove the foil and pie weights. Continue to bake the shell until golden, about 10 minutes longer. Cool completely.

Combine the remaining stevia with ½ cup water, set aside. In a double boiler, melt the chocolate. Set aside to cool slightly.

Pulse the ricotta and cream cheese in a food processor until smooth. Add the whole egg and 3 egg yolks, 1 at a time, and process until smooth. Add the cooled melted chocolate slowly and process until combined. With the machine running, add the stevia water in a thin steady stream and process until smooth.

Pour this custard into the tart shell and bake until the filling is almost set, approximately 30 minutes. Scatter the remaining ¾ cup toasted pine nuts on top of the filling. Let the tart cool completely before serving.

Almond Pecan Pie Crust

1 cup ground almonds
½ cup ground pecans
⅓ cup chopped pitted soft dates
3 tablespoons water

Preheat oven to 250 degrees F. Oil a 9-inch pie pan.

In food processor grind dates and water until smooth, stir in nut mixture until thoroughly mixed and dough-like. Shape into a ball and place on parchment or waxed paper. Flatten with palm moistened with water. Cover with another piece of paper and roll out into a circle 11-inches in diameter. Carefully remove top paper.

Invert pie pan over rolled dough and flip over so crust goes into the pan, press down gently and carefully remove paper. Trim or crimp excess crust around rim.

Turn off heat and place piecrust in oven, close door and leave until it is dry and set, approximately 30 minutes. Note: The crust will not be very dry like a flour crust, it will still be a bit sticky and quite moist.

Brownies

6 tablespoons safflower oil
2 organic eggs
½ cup 100% cocoa powder
½ cup pecan nut meal
¼ cup arrowroot powder
1 tablespoon crushed stevia leaf powder

Preheat oven to 350 degrees F. Grease an 8-inch pie pan.

Mix all ingredients and pour into pan. Bake for approximately 20 minutes until a toothpick in center comes out clean.

Raw Apple Pie

¼ cup pecans, ground
¼ cup walnuts, ground
4 medjool dates, cut in pieces
1–2 apples, chopped (try using Lady apples)
¼ teaspoon cinnamon
⅛ teaspoon nutmeg
½ teaspoon lemon juice

Combine the nut meal and dates in a food processor and blend to mix thoroughly. Place in pie pan and press out from middle to sides to form a crust.

In a bowl, combine the chopped apples and sprinkle with lemon juice, cinnamon, nutmeg and mix. Place this in the piecrust and serve.

French Vanilla Frozen Yogurt

½ cup of coconut milk (coconut and guar gum only)
2 teaspoons unflavored gelatin, softened
4 teaspoons crushed stevia leaf powder
Pinch of salt
2 organic eggs, separated
2 cups of plain unsweetened yogurt
2 tablespoons non-alcohol vanilla extract
2 organic egg whites

Heat the coconut milk to just below boiling in the top of a double boiler. Add the gelatin, stevia, and salt, and stir these ingredients until dissolved. The gelatin keeps the mix from freezing solid when put in freezer.

Beat the egg yolks until frothy and blend in a small amount of the milk mixture, stirring constantly. This is tempering the eggs. Now gradually add the yolk mixture to the milk mixture in the double boiler in a slow thin stream, stirring constantly.

Continue cooking and stirring until it begins to thicken, then set aside. When cooled to room temperature, add the yogurt and vanilla and chill for 1 hour in a refrigerator.

Beat the egg whites until they form soft peaks, gently fold them into the chilled yogurt blend. Pour into a two-quart ice cream freezer and blend to make ice cream.

Variations:

Add ⅛ teaspoon grated lemon rind and 1 tablespoon of lemon juice, omit the vanilla for a light lemon taste.

Add in 1 teaspoon of instant espresso powder to the milk mixture when cooking for coffee flavor.

Add 3 tablespoons fresh lemon juice, 2 teaspoons finely grated lemon peel and 1 tablespoon minced fresh ginger.

Add ½ cup 100% cocoa unsweetened baking chocolate pieces and crushed stevia leaf powder, to taste

Lemon Granita

3 tablespoons crushed stevia leaf powder
1 to 2 tablespoons grated lemon zest
2½ cups of water
1 cup of fresh lemon juice

Combine stevia, lemon juice, zest and water in 13 x 9 x 2 inch pan. Freeze for 1½-hours, stirring every 30 minutes to break up crystals, until evenly crystallized (mixture can be frozen in an ice-cream maker, according to manufacturer's instructions).

Chocolate Almond Torte

7 ounces 100% cocoa unsweetened chocolate, chopped
11 tablespoons unsalted butter, cut into small pieces
2 tablespoons plus 1½ teaspoons crushed stevia leaf powder
4 large organic eggs, separated and at room temperature
½ teaspoon non-alcohol vanilla extract
1 cup finely ground almonds
¼ teaspoon cream of tartar

Preheat oven to 375 degrees F and line an 8-inch spring form pan with parchment paper. Set aside.

Melt the chocolate and butter in a double boiler and add 1-tablespoon stevia. Once completely melted, remove from heat.

Meanwhile mix the egg yolks and 1-tablespoon stevia until eggs are pale and thick, approximately 2 to 3 minutes. Beat in the melted chocolate mixture and vanilla extract in a slow thin stream. Fold in the ground almonds.

In a clean bowl, beat egg whites until foamy. Add the cream of tartar and continue whisking until soft peaks form. Gradually sprinkle in the remaining 1½ teaspoons stevia and whisk until stiff peaks form.

Fold ¼ of the stiff egg whites into the chocolate batter to lighten it. Quickly fold in the rest of the whites and mix only until incorporated.

Pour the batter into the prepared pan and bake for 45 to 50 minutes or until a toothpick inserted in the center comes out mostly clean. Remove from oven and cool on a wire rack.

Note: The cake will rise during baking but falls during cooling, leaving a crisp and cracked crust. Once cool, run a spatula around the inside of the pan to release the sides

Spelt Pie Crust

Note: Spelt is wheat; celiac sufferers should not use this recipe. Candida should only eat in rotation when on maintenance.

3 tablespoon sunflower oil
2 tablespoons cool water
¼ teaspoon salt
1 cup plus 2 tablespoons spelt flour

Preheat oven to 375 degrees F.

Whisk oil, water and salt together. Stir in the flour and mix until evenly moistened.

Press into a 9-inch pie plate. Bake the empty crust for 12 minutes and fill when cool.

Option: Fill and bake as needed for filling.

Ice Cream

1 can of coconut milk
2 organic egg yolks
4 tablespoons of coconut oil, in liquid form
1 lime, juice and zest
⅔ cup water
1 packet of gelatine; enough to make 1 pint of jelly
¼–½ teaspoon crushed stevia leaf powder

Prepare the gelatine in the water according to the instructions on the packet and stir well to make sure it dissolves. Blend the coconut milk, coconut oil and egg yolks together, add the limejuice and zest and blend again. Add gelatine mixture and ¼ teaspoon stevia and blend again. Taste mixture for sweetness and add more stevia as needed.

Pour into an ice cream maker and blend for approximately 20 minutes.

Note: The gelatine mix is to stop the ice cream freezing solid in the ice cream maker. The jelly replaces the action of the sugar so that you can churn the ice cream without a disaster.

MAIN COURSES

main course: the principal dish of a meal

Main Courses

Spaghetti (Squash Noodles)

1 spaghetti squash, cooked by your method of choice (see below)
1 large yellow onion, diced
1 green bell pepper, chopped
1 red bell pepper, chopped
2 tablespoons extra virgin or cold pressed olive oil
1 20-ounce can crushed tomatoes
3–5 cloves garlic, minced
1 teaspoon basil
½ teaspoon oregano
½ teaspoon crushed red pepper flakes (optional)
1 cup grated mozzarella cheese (optional)

Heat olive oil in a skillet and add the onion, pepper and garlic. Sauté over medium heat approximately 5 minutes. Add crushed tomatoes, basil, and crushed red pepper. Simmer uncovered 15 minutes. Mix squash with the sauce. Top with grated cheese

Serves 6–8

How to Cook Spaghetti Squash

- **Bake It**—Pierce the shell several times with a large fork and place in baking dish. Cook in preheated 375 degree F oven approximately 1 hour until tender.

- **Boil It**—Boil a pot of water large enough to hold the whole squash. Drop in the squash and cook for 20 to 30 minutes, depending on its size. When a fork goes easily into the flesh, the squash is cooked.

- **Microwave It**—Cut squash in half lengthwise and remove seeds. Place cut sides up in a microwave dish with ¼ cup water. Cover with parchment paper and cook on high for 10 to 12 minutes or more. Let stand covered for 5 minutes.

Once the squash is cooked, let it cool for 10 to 20 minutes so it will be easier to handle, before cutting in half (if it wasn't already) and removing the seeds. Pull a fork lengthwise through to separate it into long strands.

Turkey and Vegetables

1 pound turkey breast, skinless
1 tablespoon extra virgin or cold pressed olive oil
1 medium onion, chopped
1 large lemon
1¼ cups lemon juice
1 bay leaf
1 cup broccoli florets
1 large zucchini, diced
1 tablespoon diced black olives

Bring a saucepan of water to a boil.

Cut turkey in thin strips. In a large skillet heat oil and cook onion and turkey until browned, approximately 5 minutes. Add in the lemon juice, bay leaf and pepper.

Cook broccoli in boiling water for 2 minutes, covered. Add diced zucchini, bring back to boil and cook approximately 3 minutes, being careful not to overcook. The vegetables should be tender but crisp. Drain.

Add broccoli and zucchini to the turkey mixture and heat through, approximately 3–4 minutes. Garnish with black olives.

Serves 4

Wild Rice Meatloaf

1 cup cooked wild rice
1½ pounds ground beef, lean
½ cup green bell pepper, chopped
½ cup red bell pepper, chopped
½ cup onion, chopped

2 garlic cloves, chopped
1 cup mozzarella cheese, grated
3 organic eggs
1 teaspoon rosemary
1 teaspoon pepper

Preheat oven to 350 degrees F.

Wash wild rice and place in boiling salted water. Boil 30 minutes or until done, drain.

In large bowl, combine wild rice with all other ingredients and mix well. Place into 9 x 4 x 3-inch pan and shape into a loaf. Bake 45 minutes.

Serves 6

Mexican Kasha Skillet

1 pound ground beef
1 cup chopped onion
¼ cup chopped celery
¼ cup chopped green bell pepper
1½ cup water
¼ cup uncooked kasha, whole or coarse
1 16-ounce can tomatoes, cut-up
Few red pepper flakes
½ teaspoon chili powder

In a skillet, cook ground beef, onion, green pepper and celery until meat is brown and vegetables are tender; drain off all but 2 tablespoons fat.

Stir in uncooked kasha to moisten grains. Add remaining ingredients and mix.

Cover and simmer for 25 to 35 minutes or until kasha is tender. Stir mixture occasionally and add extra liquid, water or tomato juice, if necessary.

Stuffed Turkey Loaf

2 pounds ground turkey
1 medium onion, finely chopped
1 tablespoon parsley
1 tablespoon chopped chives
1 clove garlic, crushed
1 tablespoon fresh tarragon
1 medium organic egg white, lightly beaten
1 medium zucchini
2 medium tomatoes
Pepper to taste
Tomato Herb Sauce (See condiments)

Preheat oven to 375 degrees F. Line a loaf pan with parchment paper. Bring a kettle of water to boil.

In a medium bowl combine turkey, onion, garlic, tarragon, chives, parsley, onion and pepper. Mix, add the egg white and mix in.

Press half the mixture in the bottom of loaf pan. Slice the zucchini thinly and arrange a layer on top of mixture. Slice tomatoes thinly and arrange a layer on top of the zucchini. Top with remaining mixture and press down firmly.

Cover with a layer of foil and place into a roasting pan. Pour enough boiling water into roasting pan to come up halfway on loaf pan.

Bake for 1 to 1½ hours; remove foil the last 20 minutes. When a skewer inserted in the center and juices run out clear, the loaf is done.

Serves 6

Crab Tortillas

¾ cup part-skim ricotta cheese
2 tablespoons finely chopped jalapeno peppers
2 tablespoons finely chopped fresh cilantro

2 tablespoons finely chopped green onion
1 tablespoon lime juice
¼ teaspoon salt
½ pound fresh crabmeat, drained and flaked
2 teaspoons butter, softened
1 head of Boston lettuce

Separate, wash and dry lettuce leaves and place the on a serving platter.

Stem and seed jalapeno peppers, chop finely. Remove stems from cilantro and chop fine. Be sure to thoroughly wash your hands after handling chilies.

Combine ricotta cheese, jalapeno, cilantro, green onion and limejuice in a small bowl; mix well. Fold in crabmeat, and fill the center of each lettuce cup.

Serves 4

Turkey Meatballs with Lemon Sauce

1 cup cooked kasha (any kind)
1 organic egg, beaten
1 teaspoon Bragg's amino acids
1 teaspoon grated lemon peel
1½ pounds ground turkey
2 tablespoons safflower oil
1 cup chicken or turkey broth
¼ cup plain unsweetened yogurt
1 tablespoon cornstarch
1 tablespoon lemon juice
1 small carrot, finely shredded
1 green onion, diced

Prepare kasha according to package directions, using broth. Combine egg, Braggs, lemon peel, turkey and kasha in a mixing bowl; blend well. Shape into 12 golf-ball size balls.

In large skillet, heat oil and brown balls on all sides. Add broth; cover and simmer 20 minutes. Use slotted spoon to transfer turkey to serving dish.

In a small bowl, combine yogurt, cornstarch, and lemon juice. Add into pan juices in skillet and cook until thickened. Add carrot and onion and cook until heated through. Pour over turkey and serve.

Serves 6

Sushi Rolls

Nori (seaweed) sheets (dried not roasted)
1 carrot, cut in thin strips
1 avocado, cut in strips lengthwise
1 cucumber, cut in thin strips lengthwise
Boston lettuce leaves
Braggs Amino Acids

Line a Nori sheet with a lettuce leaf and place cucumber and carrot strips in the middle and surround with the avocado. Lightly sprinkle with Bragg's. Roll up and eat.

Options: Add some sprouts, or cooked shrimp, or thinly sliced strips of leftover meat or pork.

Simple Turkey Meatloaf

2 pounds ground turkey
1 celery stalk, diced
1 small onion, diced
½ cup carrot, diced
2 teaspoons poultry seasoning (see condiments)
1 egg
¼ cup ground almond crumbs

Preheat oven to 350 degrees F.

Mix all ingredients together and form a loaf. Place in an ovenproof casserole dish. Bake one hour.

Serves 4–6

Turkey Burgers

1½ pounds ground turkey
1 organic egg
3 tablespoons Bragg's amino acids
2 tablespoons dried marjoram or basil
1½ teaspoons garlic powder
1½ teaspoons onion powder
Black pepper to taste

Preheat broiler.

Combine all ingredients, and form into 4–6 patties. Broil until well done, approximately 10 minutes turning once during cooking.

Serves 4–6

Lamb Kebabs

1 pound lean lamb
4 small zucchini
2 lemons
Rind from one lemon
1 red onion
2 tablespoons cold pressed or extra virgin olive oil
1 clove garlic, crushed
1 teaspoon cinnamon
1 teaspoon ground ginger
½ teaspoon ground cumin
½ teaspoon ground coriander

Preheat broiler or barbeque grill. Trim lamb of any fat and cut into 1-inch pieces. Soak bamboo skewers in water.

In a small bowl combine lemon rind and juice from one lemon, olive oil, garlic, cinnamon, ginger, cumin and coriander. Add in lamb and toss to coat. Refrigerate for 30 minutes up to 2 hours. The longer you refrigerate the deeper the flavor.

Cut remaining lemon in 8 pieces. Cut the onion into halves, and each half in thirds. Separate all pieces. Peel the zucchinis removing evenly spaced strips leaving peel strips between. Cut into ½ inch wide rounds.

Remove lamb from marinade and skewer, alternate with a zucchini piece and an onion, and add one lemon wedge onto each skewer.

Broil or grill for 10 minutes, basting with marinade often and turning until cooked.

Serves 4 to 6

Kasha and Shrimp Jambalaya

Note: the use of rice in this dish makes it a rotational food only.

¾ cup whole kasha
½ cup brown rice
2 tablespoons vegetable oil
¾ cup chorizo, sliced
½ cup sliced celery
½ cup diced onion
½ cup diced green bell pepper
1 14½-ounce can diced tomatoes with chilies
1 pound medium-sized shrimp, cooked, shelled and cleaned
2¾ cups boiling water

In a large skillet over high heat, cook and stir kasha and rice until toasted, approximately 3 minutes, remove to a bowl.

Add oil to skillet and heat until hot; stir in chorizo, celery, onion and bell pepper; cook and stir over medium high heat until onion is tender, approximately 5 minutes.

Add kasha and rice mixture and boiling water. Cover and simmer until kasha and rice are tender, 8 to 10 minutes.

Stir in tomatoes, and shrimp; cover and cook until heated through, about 2 minutes.

Serve 4 to 6

Pork Noodles

1 pound pork, cut into strips
2 tablespoons Bragg's amino acids
¼ teaspoon black ground pepper
5 tablespoons coconut oil, liquefied
1 large onion, thinly sliced
2 large cloves garlic, minced
1 teaspoon ginger, minced
1 red pepper, seeded and thinly sliced
¼ pound snow peas
¾ pound Soba noodles, cooked
2 teaspoons curry powder
¼ cup fresh coriander leaves OR 2 minced scallions

In a bowl, marinate pork with Bragg's and black pepper for 10 minutes.

In wok or large skillet heat 4 tablespoons of oil over medium-high heat and add onion, garlic, and gingerroot. Cook 1 minute then add pepper strips and snow peas cooking until crisp-tender-about 1 minute. Remove and set aside. Wipe pan dry and reheat on high heat.

Add remaining 1 tablespoon of coconut oil and stir-fry pork for 30 seconds then reduce heat slightly and add curry powder. Stir-fry until aromatic and pork is cooked.

Add vegetable mixture and cooked noodles and mix in Bragg's, coriander leaves (or green onions). Taste for spices and adjust.

Serves 4

Seared Halibut

4 halibut steaks, skinned
2 tablespoons chives, minced
½ teaspoon cornstarch dissolved in 2 tablespoons water
2 medium red onions
6 shallots

2 tablespoons lemon juice
3 tablespoons extra virgin or cold pressed olive oil
⅔ cup fish stock
1¼ teaspoons crushed stevia leaf powder

Peel onions and shallots and thinly slice. Mix in a small bowl with 2 tablespoons lemon juice.

In a skillet heat the oil and sauté onions and shallots until softened, approximately 3 minutes. Add in stevia and turn heat to high. Add in stock and season with pepper to taste. Bring to boil, reduce heat to simmer and cook for 8 minutes or until the sauce is thickened and slightly reduced.

Heat another skillet, coated with oil, and cook the fish steaks on each side briefly to sear. Reduce heat and cook for 4 minutes, turn over and cook an additional four minutes. Place on paper toweling to drain but keep warm.

Stir cornstarch into onion sauce and stir to thicken. Season to taste. Serve Halibut on top of onion mixture.

Serves 4

Kasha Stuffed Italian Peppers

1 tablespoon vegetable oil
1½ cups chopped onions
½ cup diced carrot
1 cup whole kasha
¼ teaspoon ground black pepper
2 tablespoons chopped fresh dill weed
1 cup crumbled feta cheese
3 green and red bell peppers, cut lengthwise in halves and seeded

Preheat oven to 350 degrees F.

Heat oil in a large skillet over medium-high heat, add onions and carrot; cook and stir until onion is tender, about 5 minutes. Stir in kasha, salt and black pepper. Cook while stirring until kasha is lightly browned approximately 5 minutes.

Stir in 1½ cups water and the dill; cover and simmer until water is absorbed, about 10 minutes. Stir in half of the feta. Spoon into each pepper half, dividing evenly.

Sprinkle with remaining feta. Arrange peppers in baking dish. Add ¾ cup water to the dish and cover tightly with foil. Bake about 30 minutes until peppers are tender.

Serves 6

Turkey Chili

4 cups cooked turkey meat, cubed in 1 inch pieces
2 cups chopped onion
4 garlic cloves, chopped fine
1½ cup chopped green pepper
¼ cup cold pressed or extra virgin olive oil
2 16-ounce cans tomatoes, crushed
2 15-ounce cans kidney beans, drained (or 1 can kidney beans 1 can black or pinto beans)
2 tablespoons tomato paste
¾ cup chicken stock
1 teaspoon cumin seed
1 teaspoon oregano
⅛ teaspoon ground cloves
1 tablespoon dried red pepper flakes
2 tablespoons chili powder
Pepper to taste

In a large saucepan, cook the onion and green pepper over medium high heat, stirring until golden, about 5 minutes.

Add the garlic, chili powder, cumin, oregano, cloves, and pepper flakes and cook while stirring, for a minute or two more. Add a bit more olive oil if needed.

Add tomatoes, tomato paste, stock, beans, and turkey meat. Bring mixture to a simmer, taste and add pepper, if needed. Simmer, uncovered, for an hour.

If the taste is too sharp and acid, you can add ⅛ teaspoon stevia crushed leaf powder, if desired.

Serves 8

Olive Chicken

3 chicken fryers cut in serving pieces
4 tablespoons cold pressed or extra virgin olive oil
1 teaspoon freshly ground black pepper
½ cup pimentos
2 teaspoons oregano
2 large onions, coarsely chopped
1 large green bell pepper, diced large chucks
3 cloves garlic, minced
1½ cups olives, stuffed with pimentos or roasted red pepper (olives must be citrus acid brined)
1½ cups whole canned tomatoes, cut into medium pieces

Wash and dry chicken, place in shallow baking dish, sprinkle with black pepper and oregano. Add onions, bell pepper, garlic, and olives. Add the pimentos and tomatoes along with liquid and olive oil.

Cover and marinate in refrigerator several hours or overnight.

Bake in 350 degree F oven for 1½ hours.

Serves 12

Thai Chicken Stir-Fry

4 chicken breasts, boneless and skinless
8 shallots, sliced
3 tablespoons sesame oil
2 cloves garlic, finely chopped
1 inch piece of ginger, peeled and grated
1 green chili pepper, seeded and veins removes, thinly sliced
1 red bell pepper, thinly sliced

3 zucchini, thinly sliced
2 tablespoons ground almonds
1 teaspoon ground cinnamon
1 tablespoon oyster sauce (see condiments section)
¼ cup grated fresh coconut or unsweetened shredded coconut
Black pepper, coarse ground

Cut chicken in thin slices. In a wok or large skillet heat oil, add chicken, black pepper and stir-fry for 4 minutes. Add shallots, ginger, and chili pepper and cook another 2 minutes.

Add bell pepper, zucchini and cook for approximately 1 minute. Add garlic, almonds, cinnamon, oyster sauce and coconut. Stir-fry for 1 minute and remove from heat.

Serves 4

Millet with Shrimp

1-pound shrimp, shelled and cleaned
¼ cup sliced green onion
2 tablespoons butter
1½ cups chicken stock
¼ teaspoon ground peppercorns, black or colored
⅓ cup unsalted roasted cashews
3 tablespoons Bragg's amino acids
2 teaspoons cornstarch
1 teaspoon grated fresh ginger root
⅛ teaspoon crushed stevia leaf powder
¼ teaspoon red pepper flakes
2 tablespoons coconut oil, liquefied
6–8 ounces fresh pea pods
1 medium tomato, peeled, seeded & chopped
⅔ cup hulled millet

In a large saucepan cook the millet grains and green onion in butter until lightly browned and onion is tender. Stir in chicken broth and add pepper. Bring to boil and reduce heat; simmer covered for 15 minutes. Remove from heat and stir in cashews. Keep warm while stir-frying shrimp.

In a separate bowl stir Bragg's into cornstarch; add ginger root, stevia and red pepper flakes. Set aside.

Preheat a wok or large skillet over high heat; add cooking oil. Stir-fry shrimp 1 to 2 minutes or just until shrimp are done-curled and pink. Do not overcook shrimp, as they will rubberize. Push shrimp away from center of wok or skillet.

Stir cornstarch mixture in center of wok or skillet, cook and stir until thickened and bubbly. Add in pea pods and tomato. Cover and cook 1 minute. Serve over millet mixture.

Serves 4

Yaki Soba Noodles

1½ pounds beef or pork, cut into small chunks
1 large green bell pepper
1 medium head Chinese cabbage
1 package Soba noodles
2 tablespoons safflower oil
6 green onions or 2 medium yellow onions
2 tablespoons Bragg's amino acids

In large saucepan cook noodles, drain and hold warm.

Stir-fry meat in a skillet with the oil then remove and set aside. Make sure enough oil remains in pan to cook vegetables.

Cut cabbage into chunks and the pepper and onions into strips. In skillet over medium heat cook cabbage then remove from skillet and cook onions and peppers together.

Mix noodles, meat, and vegetables together and sprinkle with Bragg's and toss.

Serves 4 or 5

Peppered Blackened Fish

4 fish steaks, halibut or other firm white fish
1 teaspoon ground black pepper
½ teaspoon ground white pepper
1 tablespoon paprika
1 teaspoon thyme
¼ teaspoon allspice
1 teaspoon cayenne
4 tablespoons butter
3 tablespoons sunflower oil

Preheat broiler or grill.

In a flat dish, mix paprika, black and white pepper, cayenne, allspice and thyme. In a small saucepan, melt butter and add oil.

Brush fish steaks with melted butter on both sides and then dredge in the spice mixture coating all sides.

Broil or grill approximately 10 minutes per side. Baste fish with remaining butter and oil mixture.

Serves 4

Lamb & Pear Tagine

2 large onions, peeled and sliced
2 pounds lean lamb, leg or shoulder—cut into 1-inch cubes
4 pears, peeled cored and cut into 1-inch chunks
½ cup golden raisins
½ cup silvered almonds
1 tablespoon olive oil
1 teaspoon cumin
1 teaspoon ground coriander
1 teaspoon ground ginger
1 teaspoon cinnamon
1 teaspoon black pepper

Water, to cover the meat
Salt, to taste

In a large saucepan, gently fry the onion in olive oil until soft. Add in the meat and cook until browned then add the spices and water to just cover the meat. Cover and simmer gently until the meat is tender, about 1½ to 2 hours.

Add the pears to the cooked meat along with the raisins and almonds and cook for a further 5 minutes or until the pears are soft.

Serves 4

Broiled Chicken with Garlic Lime

4 boneless chicken breast halves
Juice of ½ lime
¼ cup vegetable broth
1 garlic clove, sliced

Preheat broiler.

Place chicken in a shallow baking pan; pour limejuice and broth over the chicken, turning pieces to coat. Sprinkle slices of garlic over chicken. Place the pan 5–6 inches from heat for 15–20 minutes.

Serves 4

Skewered Salmon

1 pound salmon, skinned and cut into 1½-inch pieces
1 tablespoon cornstarch
6 tablespoons extra virgin or cold pressed olive oil
4 tomatoes seeded and cut in chunks
1 small organic egg white, beaten
1 red bell pepper
1 green bell pepper
¼ cucumber, peeled, seeded and chopped
8 basil leaves, torn into large pieces

2 tablespoons lemon juice
Pepper

Preheat broiler or grill. Soak wooden skewers.

Place salmon on a dish and sprinkle with cornstarch, pepper on one side. Add beaten egg white and toss to coat. Chill for 15 minutes.

Clean bell peppers and cut into 1½-inch pieces. Skewer the salmon pieces with pieces of bell pepper between each on soaked skewers. Set aside.

In a blender or food processor place seeded tomatoes, cucumber, basil leaves, 2 tablespoons lemon juice, 6 tablespoons olive oil and pepper and pulse to a coarse chop.

Broil salmon or grill for 10 minutes basting frequently with oil. Serve the salmon with sauce over top.

Serves 4

Southwest Style Chicken

¼ cup cold pressed or extra virgin olive oil
1–3½ pound frying chicken, cut in pieces
1 red bell pepper, seeded and chopped
2 cloves of garlic, crushed
1 small jalapeno, seeded and veins removed, chopped
1 teaspoon ground cumin
1 large tomato, peeled and chopped
1 tablespoon lemon juice
1-pound cooked chickpeas, pinto or black beans (or a combination)

Boil water in a saucepan. At each end of tomato score in an X, plunge tomato into saucepan of boiling water for 20–30 seconds, remove and set aside to cool. When cool peel off tomato skin and chop tomato.

In a large frying pan over medium heat, heat the olive oil, add the chicken and lightly season with pepper; cook for 5 min browning on each side. Remove from pan.

In the same pan, over medium heat, sauté the onion, bell pepper, jalapeno, and garlic until the onion is soft, do not brown. Stir in cumin, tomato, lemon juice, and add the beans.

Return the browned chicken, cover and simmer over medium-low heat for 20 minutes.

Remove cover and cook 10 minutes more, or until chicken is tender. Taste and adjust seasoning.

Serves 4

Soba Noodle Pork Stir Fry

1 6-ounce package soba noodles
4 boneless center cut pork chops, cut in strips
1 medium yellow onion
1 green bell pepper
1 red bell pepper
1 can water chestnuts, drained
1 cup bean sprouts
½ cup sweet peas
1 tablespoon Chinese five spice
2 tablespoons Braggs amino acids
3 tablespoons coconut oil, liquified
1 stalk of green onion sliced thin, white and green portion

Cook noodles in large pot of boiling salted water until almost tender but still al dente (firm to bite). Drain well, and return to pot to keep warm.

While the noodles are cooking, season pork with pepper and five-spice powder. Heat 1 tablespoon coconut oil in medium skillet over high heat. Add in pork strips and stir-fry until cooked through, approximately 2 minutes. Set aside, keeping warm.

Add remaining 2 tablespoons oil to skillet and add onions and stir-fry just until soft and transparent, approximately 30 seconds, add in bell pepper and stir-fry for 30 seconds. Push vegetables to the sides of pan and add Braggs to bottom center of pan; push vegetables back to center, add water chestnuts, stir and cook another 30 seconds to heat through.

Add pork back to the skillet with the onions and peppers and cook while stirring constantly about 1 minute to heat through, toss in peas, bean sprouts and noodles, toss thoroughly but gently just to mix.

Remove from heat and place into serving bowl, sprinkle top with green onions

Serves 4

Belled Shrimp

1 pound medium shrimp, peeled and cleaned
1 medium red bell pepper, seeded
1 medium green bell pepper, seeded
½ stick unsalted butter
½ bunch cilantro, finely chopped
2 garlic cloves, crushed

Place shrimp in large mixing bowl; add cilantro leaves, garlic and shrimp.

Cut bell peppers into thin slices lengthwise.

Melt butter in a skillet, add shrimp mixture and stir fry for approximately 3–5 minutes, just until shrimp start to pink and curl. Do not overcook the shrimp, as they will rubberize. Add in bell pepper and cook for another 3–5 minutes.

Serves 4

Spanakopita

3 tablespoons cold pressed or extra virgin olive oil
1 onion, chopped
2 large or 3–4 small yellow squash, sliced very thin lengthwise
½ cup chopped green onions, greens and whites
3 cloves garlic, minced
2 pounds baby spinach, trimmed, rough chopped
½ lemon, juiced
2 organic eggs, lightly beaten
12 ounces crumbled fresh feta cheese

1 tablespoon coriander seeds, toasted and ground
½ teaspoon fresh grated nutmeg
½ pound unsalted butter, melted
¼ cup finely chopped fresh oregano
¼ cup finely chopped fresh chives
Pepper

Preheat oven to 350 degrees F. Brush 2 baking sheets with melted butter.

Heat olive oil in a large skillet over medium heat. Sauté onions and garlic until soft. Add the spinach and season with pepper; cook until the spinach wilts, about 2 minutes. Add lemon juice then remove from heat and set aside.

In a medium bowl, beat the eggs with feta, coriander, and nutmeg. Fold in the cooled spinach mixture and blend well.

Make a layer of the squash and do not overlap. Place a teaspoon of filling near the widest end of the slice about ¼ inch from the edge. Fold the end over the filling and roll up, making sure the loose end is underneath. Brush the top with butter. Repeat until all the filling and squash strips are used.

Bake for 20 minutes until the squash are cooked and golden.

Serve hot, warm or cold.

Serves 4

Stuffed Leg of Lamb

1 leg of lamb, boned and butterflied; approximately 3 ½-pounds
2 tablespoons olive oil
2 cloves garlic, minced
1 tablespoon chopped fresh oregano leaves
1 tablespoon chopped fresh basil leaves
Fresh ground pepper
1 whole bulb garlic
4 ounces feta cheese, crumbled
1 red bell pepper, roasted, skinned, and cut lengthwise into ¼ inch strips
12 to 15 whole fresh basil leaves

Place bell pepper under broiler and turn to roast all sides, until blackened. Remove peppers and place in a bowl of ice water. Remove the blackened skin under water.

In a small bowl, mix the olive oil, garlic, oregano and chopped basil and pepper to taste. Pour this over the lamb, which is in a baking dish. Cover with foil, and let sit at room temperature for up to 2 hours or in the refrigerator for as long as 24 hours.

Preheat the oven to 400 degrees F.

Slice ¼ inch off the top of a garlic bulb and brush with olive oil. Wrap in a piece of foil and bake for 1 hour. Let cool to room temperature.

Holding the root end of the garlic head, squeeze the soft garlic into a bowl. Add the feta and a little freshly ground pepper and mix until creamy. Bring the lamb to room temperature if refrigerated. It will take 45 minutes to 1 hour.

Preheat the oven to 500 degrees F. Remove meat from marinade, reserve ¼ cup marinade.

Score the meat on one side, to help it roll more easily, and place this side down. Place the roasted pepper strips in the middle leaving a 1-inch border around the edges. Place the whole basil leaves on top. Gently spread the feta-garlic mixture on top of the basil leaves. Beginning with one long side, roll the lamb up jellyroll fashion.

Secure by tying clean cotton twine around both ends and in the middle. Place back in roasting pan and pour over a ¼ cup of the marinade. Roast in the oven for 10 minutes.

Turn temperature down to 425 degrees F and roast until meat thermometer registers 160 degrees F, approximately 35 to 40 minutes. Remove from oven and let sit for 15 minutes to allow the juices to redistribute through the meat before slicing.

Serves 6

No Noodle Lasagna

2 pounds lean ground beef
2 tablespoons cold pressed or extra virgin olive oil
½ small onion, diced
½ red or green bell pepper, diced

15 ounces ricotta cheese
2 organic eggs, beaten slightly
8 ounces tomato sauce
3 tablespoons tomato paste
2 teaspoons dried basil
2 teaspoons dried marjoram
2 teaspoons dried oregano
1 teaspoon dried sage
½ teaspoon fennel seed
Fresh chopped parsley
2 medium zucchini, sliced lengthwise
1 pound spinach, steamed
Pepper to taste
2 cloves garlic, crushed
8 ounces mozzarella cheese, sliced thin

Preheat oven to 325 degrees F.

Brown the meat in 2 tablespoons olive oil. When meat is nearly done, add the onions and bell pepper and sauté until the onions begin to soften. Add garlic and continue cooking until onions are transparent. Add tomato sauce and paste and mix well; add seasonings and simmer.

Beat the eggs and ricotta together with some fresh chopped parsley; add salt and pepper to taste.

Coat a baking dish with olive oil. Place a layer of zucchini in the bottom of the pan. Spread ½ of the meat mixture and top and layer with sliced mozzarella. Spread ricotta mixture next and top with spinach. Cover with another layer of the zucchini and remaining meat mixture, top with remaining cheese. Bake at 325-degrees F. until the cheese is bubbly and golden—about 35 to 45 minutes.

Serves 8

Eggplant and Zucchini Lasagna

1 15-ounce container ricotta cheese
1 teaspoon dried basil
1 teaspoon dried oregano

1 tablespoon chopped fresh flat-leaf parsley
½ teaspoon ground black pepper
1 pound zucchini, sliced lengthwise ¼ inch thick
1 pound eggplant, peeled and sliced ¼ inch thick
26 ounces tomato sauce
2 cups thin sliced mozzarella cheese

Pre-heat oven to 375°F. Grease a 13 x 9-inch baking dish with olive oil.

In a large bowl, combine the ricotta cheese, basil, oregano, parsley, and pepper. Layer in half of the zucchini, top with ricotta cheese mixture, add a layer of eggplant, spoon on ½ of the tomato sauce, and layer with sliced mozzarella cheese. Repeat in the same order, leaving off the top mozzarella layer. Bake for about 40 minutes.

Remove from the oven and top evenly with a layer of mozzarella cheese. Bake for an additional 5 to 8 minutes, until the cheese is melted and lightly brown. Remove from the oven and let rest at least 15 minutes before serving.

Serves 4 to 6

Veal Scaloppini with Lentils

1¼ cups green lentils, rinsed
4 tablespoons unsalted butter
Fresh ground pepper
3 ½ cups chicken stock
1 bay leaf
½ cup finely diced carrot
½ cup finely diced zucchini
½ cup finely diced onion
½ cup finely diced celery
8 slices of veal, 2-ounces each, pounded thin
½ cup plus 1 tablespoon cold pressed or extra virgin olive oil
2 tablespoons lemon juice
2 tablespoon chopped parsley

Preheat the oven to 300 degrees F.

In a medium saucepan, melt 2 tablespoons of butter. Stir in the lentils; season lightly with pepper. Add the chicken stock, bay leaf and bring to a boil. Simmer over low heat 30 minutes.

Meanwhile, in a medium skillet, melt the remaining 2 tablespoons of butter. Add the diced carrot, zucchini, onion and celery. Season with pepper and cook over low heat stirring often until just tender but not browned, about 10 minutes.

Drain lentils over a bowl, reserving the cooking liquid. Discard the bay leaf. Return lentils to the saucepan and pour in ½ cup of the cooking liquid. Stir in the vegetables and season with pepper.

Season 4 of the veal slices with pepper. Heat ½ cup of the olive oil in a large skillet, add the veal and brown, about 2 minutes per side. Serve over lentils.

Serves 4

Chicken Satay

4 large boneless, skinless chicken breasts
½ teaspoon ground cumin
1¼ teaspoon garlic powder
⅓ cup almond butter
3 tablespoons extra virgin or cold pressed olive oil
3 tablespoons lemon juice
1 medium onion, sliced

Preheat broiler.

Cube chicken into 1-inch pieces. Combine cumin and 2 tablespoons of the oil with lemon juice in a bowl, add chicken and toss to coat. Set aside to marinate for 10 minutes.

Heat 1 tablespoon of oil in a skillet and sauté the onion until golden. Stir in water, garlic powder, and 1 tablespoon lemon juice. Bring mixture to a boil and remove pan from heat, stir in almond butter until melted. Keep warm.

Place chicken on broiler rack and cook approximately 5 minutes per side until the juices run clear and the chicken is thoroughly cooked. Serve with sauce over the top.

Serves 4

Baked Chicken

4 chicken quarters with skin
2 tablespoons sunflower oil
16 small whole onions, peeled
3 stalk celery, sliced
1 14-ounce can red kidney beans
4 medium tomatoes, quartered
1 cup chicken stock
2 tablespoons chopped parsley
1 teaspoon paprika

In an oven proof skillet or casserole heat the oil and brown the chicken. Remove from pan and set aside. In the same pan add the celery and cook 2–3 minutes then stir in beans, tomatoes half the parsley and season with pepper to taste. Return chicken to pan. Sprinkle with paprika.

Cook in oven for 25 minutes. Sprinkle with remaining parsley to serve.

Serves 4

Shepherd's Pie

1½ pounds ground beef or turkey
1 cup onion, finely chopped
¼ teaspoon garlic powder
1 medium carrot, finely chopped
1 package of frozen peas, thawed
1 small head of cauliflower
3 tablespoons butter, melted

Preheat oven to 350 degrees F. Bring a saucepan of water to boil.

Cook cauliflower in boiling water until fork tender, drain and set aside. In a skillet, lightly coated with 1 tablespoon butter, cook the onions until soft and transparent, add the carrot and cook until tender, remove from pan and set aside, keeping warm. Add the ground meat to skillet and brown, drain off the fat. Add the ground meat mixture to a baking dish, stir in the onion mixture and peas.

In a bowl mash the cauliflower and add 2 tablespoons of butter slowly until a mixture similar to mashed potatoes. Spread completely over top of the meat mixture and cook in oven about 25 minutes until browned.

Serves 4–6

Garlic and Mustard Chicken

4 skinless boneless chicken breasts
3 cloves of garlic, finely chopped
2 tablespoons dry mustard
¼ cup lemon juice
¾ cup olive oil

In a bowl, combine garlic, mustard powder and lemon juice. Whisk in olive oil slowly. Add chicken and coat pieces well. Cover and refrigerate.

Preheat oven to 350 degrees F.

Place chicken in baking dish and pour on marinade. Bake for 45 minutes, turning after 25 minutes.

Serves 4

Oven Baked Ribs

4 pounds pork spareribs
Rub:
4 teaspoons paprika
2 teaspoons salt
2 teaspoons onion powder

2 teaspoons fresh ground black pepper
1 teaspoons cayenne

Sauce:
6 ounces tomato paste
1 medium onion, chopped fine
1 teaspoon dry mustard
2 cloves garlic, minced
1 tablespoon stevia crushed leaf powder
1 large lemon, juiced

Preheat oven to 250 degrees F.

In a small bowl combine the rub ingredients and rub the ribs thoroughly. Place ribs in foil and seal and place in a baking dish. Bake for 3½–4 hours.

Meanwhile, in a saucepan combine the ingredients for the sauce and cook until thick. Refrigerate until the 4th hour of the ribs cooking time.

Open the ribs packet and drain excess liquid. Coat the ribs with the sauce, do not reseal but leave open and bake in the oven for another hour uncovered.

Remove ribs and place on broiler pan, crisp under broiler or place on grill for 1–2 minutes.

Serves 4

Sesame Chicken

4 chicken quarters, skinless
½ cup plain unsweetened yogurt
2 teaspoons curry paste (see condiments section)
1 tablespoon sesame seeds
1 small lemon, juiced and grated rind

Preheat broiler. Score the chicken and set aside.

In a small bowl, mix the yogurt, lemon juice, rind and curry paste until smooth.

Place chicken on a cookie sheet and cover with the mixture, ensuring both sides are well covered.

Broil 12–15 minutes, turning once, until golden brown. Sprinkle with sesame seeds and serve.

Serves 4

Lemon Sauced Chicken

4 skinless, boneless chicken breasts
2 tablespoons olive oil
4 tablespoons butter
⅓ cup chicken broth
2 teaspoons fresh lemon juice
8 slices lemon, ⅛ inch thick
Chopped fresh parsley

Put a platter in the oven to warm, turning oven to 200 degrees F.

Flatten chicken breasts slightly with a mallet or the side of a cleaver between two sheets of parchment or waxed paper.

Heat oil and butter in a large, heavy skillet over moderately high heat. Add half the chicken pieces and cook approximately 3 minutes on each side, until lightly browned. Remove to warm platter and repeat with remaining chicken.

Add chicken broth to skillet and stir to release brown bits from bottom of pan. Increase heat to high; add fresh lemon juice and lemon slices. Cook approximately 2 minutes, until sauce is slightly syrupy. Layer chicken with lemon slices and pour on sauce

Serves 4

Southern Style "Fried" Chicken

4 skinless chicken leg and thigh pieces
½ cup buckwheat groats
1 tablespoon sesame seeds

1 tablespoon rosemary, fresh chopped
1 organic egg white
¼ teaspoon pepper

Preheat oven to 400 degrees F.

In a bowl, mix the groats, sesame seeds, and rosemary with ¼ teaspoon pepper.

Brush each piece of chicken with egg white and coat in groat mixture. Place on a cookie sheet and bake for 40 minutes or until the juices run clear when pricked.

Serves 4

Grilled Indian Shrimp

16 large shrimp, peeled and cleaned
2 tablespoons butter
½ teaspoon ground turmeric
¼ teaspoon ground ginger
¼ teaspoon ground cumin
¼ teaspoon ground coriander
½ lemon, juiced

Preheat the broiler with the pan 3 inches from heat.

Melt butter in a small skillet and add spices and lemon juice. Place shrimp in a single layer in a shallow baking pan and brush with butter mixture.

Broil for 2–3 minutes, turn, brush again with butter mixture and broil additional 2–4 minutes.

Serves 2

Soufflé

2 organic egg whites
½ teaspoon cream of tartar
1 cup ricotta cheese

1 organic egg yolk
⅛ teaspoon stevia crushed leaf powder

Preheat oven to 300 degrees F. Butter a 9-inch round cake pan.

Beat egg whites until frothy, add cream of tartar and continue beating until stiff peaks form.

In another bowl combine egg yolk, ricotta and stevia, mix well. Fold gently into egg whites. Pour soufflé mixture into buttered cake pan and bake for 25 to 30 minutes.

When cooked, turn on broiler and brown soufflé.

Serves 2

Irish Stew

12 lamb shoulder slices, trimmed of fat
2 pounds turnip, peeled and sliced
4 large onions, peeled and sliced
Freshly ground black pepper
1 teaspoon dried thyme

In a deep saucepan place alternate layers of turnip, onion and lamb slices, seasoning with pepper and thyme as you layer. Finish with a layer of turnips and onions.

Pour in enough water just to cover the top layer, cover saucepan and simmer for 1½ to 2 hours. Add a few tablespoons of boiling water from time to time to prevent stew from burning. Taste and add salt, if needed, before serving.

Serves 4–6

Broiled Rock Cornish Game Hens

2 Rock Cornish game hens
1 teaspoon extra virgin or cold pressed olive oil
2 tablespoons butter
½ lemon, grated rind

1 tablespoon lemon juice
1 clove garlic, chopped
4 sprigs fresh tarragon
Pepper

Preheat broiler.

Clean hens and place breast side down on a cutting board. Split at the backbone with kitchen scissors and lay bird flat, press to flatten as much as possible; season with pepper.

Place a twig of tarragon under the skin of each breast half. Brush with oil and place under broiler for approximately 15 minutes until lightly browned.

While hens are broiling, melt butter in a small saucepan and add lemon rind, lemon juice, garlic and season with pepper.

Remove hens from the broiler and thoroughly brush both sides with the mixture and place back under broiler for another 15 minutes, turning once and basting every 5 minutes to keep moist.

Serves 2

Chicken Curry

3 pounds chicken pieces, skinless and boneless
1 teaspoon paprika
4 tablespoons butter
5 tablespoons coconut oil, liquefied
1 onion, peeled and chopped
1½ teaspoons curry powder
2 cups chicken broth
⅓ cup sliced blanched almonds, toasted
½ cup golden raisins, soaked approximately 20 minutes in stock to hydrate
Freshly ground white pepper

Sprinkle chicken pieces with pepper and paprika.

Heat coconut oil in skillet and sauté chicken until browned. Remove from pan set aside, keeping warm.

Wipe out pan and heat butter in skillet, add onion and cook until onion is soft. Stir in the curry powder and pour in the stock, add raisins.

Add the chicken back to the pan, cover and simmer for 40 minutes until chicken is tender.

Remove chicken and set aside, keep warm. Reduce the liquid by boiling hard for 10 minutes. Replace chicken portions, reheat and serve sprinkled with almonds.

Serves 4–6

Yogurt Crusted Chicken

4 boneless, skinless chicken breasts
1 clove garlic, crushed
1-inch piece ginger root, peeled and finely chopped
1 green chili, seeded and finely chopped
6 tablespoons plain unsweetened yogurt
1 tablespoon tomato paste
1 teaspoon ground turmeric
1 teaspoon Garam Marsala (see condiments section)
1 tablespoon limejuice
Pepper

Preheat oven to 375 degrees F.

In a small bowl combine garlic, ginger, chili, yogurt, tomato paste, turmeric, Garam Marsala, lime juice and pepper to taste.

Place chicken breast on a cookie sheet and brush with the yogurt mixture. Turn over and coat other side.

Bake in oven 35 minutes until cooked through. Drain on paper towels.

Serve hot, or chill for 1 hour and serve cold on a salad.

Serves 4

German Style Roast Pork

2¼ pound leg of pork (fresh ham), score fat in diamond pattern
Fresh ground black pepper to taste
6 cloves garlic
2 onions, peeled and chopped
2 carrots, peeled and chopped
1 turnip, peeled and chopped
¼ cup vegetable stock
2 teaspoons cornstarch, dissolved in a small amount of stock

Preheat oven to 400 degrees F.

Rub the meat with pepper and stick the garlic cloves into the fat scores. Bring water to boil in a roasting pan on stove top, put in the pork with the fat side down. Roast in oven for 20 minutes.

Remove from oven and place a rack in the roasting pan to elevate the pork and place it fat side up. Return to oven and roast another 30 minutes.

Now add the vegetables to pan and cook another 20 minutes. If/when necessary add more water to roasting pan.

Ten minutes before the end of cooking time, brush the fat with some vegetable stock. Remove from oven cover with foil and let rest for 10 minutes before carving.

Serves 4

Grilled Scallop Skewers

12 medium large dry pack scallops
1 red bell pepper
1 green bell pepper
1 yellow bell pepper
½ teaspoon dried dill
4 tablespoons sunflower oil
6 slices of uncured prosciutto
Juice and grated rind of ½ lemon

Soak skewers in water

Mix in a bowl rind and juice from lemon with sunflower oil and dried dill. Add the scallops and mix. Marinate for 1–2 hours in refrigerator.

Cut and clean the bell peppers, removing all ribs and cut into 1-inch pieces. Cut each proscuitto slice in half.

Preheat broiler or heat barbeque grill.

Remove scallops from marinade, wrap a piece of proscuitto around each scallop and put onto a skewer. Add a piece of each color of bell pepper followed by another bacon wrapped scallop, until you have 3 scallops per skewer.

Broil or barbeque skewers for approximately 5 minutes and baste frequently with leftover marinade.

Serves 4

Spice Crusted Chicken Breast

4 boneless skinless chicken breast halves, slightly flattened to even thickness
1 tablespoon ground coriander
1 tablespoon ground cumin
1 teaspoon freshly ground black pepper
2 teaspoons coconut oil

Preheat broiler and lightly oil broiler pan.

In a small skillet over medium heat toast the coriander, cumin and pepper stirring constantly for approximately 45 seconds or until you can smell the spices. Transfer immediately to a bowl and set aside.

Brush both sides of chicken with oil and coat with spice mixture and broil 4–5 minutes per side.

Serves 4

Lemon Chicken Kebabs

4 skinless, boneless chicken breasts
¼ cup extra virgin or cold pressed olive oil
2 tablespoons fresh lemon juice
3 cloves garlic, crushed
½ teaspoon coarsely cracked black pepper

Preheat broiler or grill. Soak skewers in water.

Cut chicken into bite-sized pieces, approximately 1-inch cubes. In small bowl combine oil, lemon juice, garlic and pepper. Add chicken and toss to coat. Leave in marinade 15 minutes.

Place 3–4 pieces per skewer and place under broiler or on grill, baste frequently with marinade and broil for 5 minutes or grill 12–15 minutes.

Serves 4

Pork with Fennel

4 lean pork chops
1 teaspoon grated lemon rind
4 scallions, finely chopped
2 cups lemon juice
1 tablespoon extra virgin or cold pressed olive oil
1 fennel bulb, trimmed and thinly sliced
1 tablespoon cornstarch
Fresh ground pepper to taste

Trim pork chops of excess fat and using a small, sharp knife make a slit from one side of the chop to make a pocket for stuffing. Mix the rind, scallions and pepper in a bowl. Stuff the chops with this mixture.

In a large skillet, fry the chops on each side until golden brown, about 2–3 minutes. Add the sliced fennel and lemon juice and bring to a boil, reduce heat to a simmer and cook for 20 minutes until meat is tender and cooked.

Remove chops from pan and set aside keeping warm. Add cornstarch to 2 tablespoons water and mix well then add to liquid in the pan and cook stirring until thickened. Serve this over the chops.

Serves 4

Oven Roasted Beef Stew

¼ cup coconut oil, liquefied
1½ pounds boneless beef chuck, cut into 1½-inch cubes
12 ounces small white boiling onions, peeled
1 pound tomatoes, peeled, seeded, and chopped
3 garlic cloves, minced
2½ tablespoons chopped fresh thyme or 1 teaspoon dried thyme
2½ tablespoons chopped fresh rosemary or 1 teaspoon dried rosemary
2½ tablespoons chopped fresh oregano or 1 teaspoon dried oregano
1 bay leaf, crumbled
1 teaspoon ground cumin
2 cups vegetable juice
Freshly ground pepper

Preheat oven to 350 degrees F. Boil water in a saucepan. Cut an X in the tomato skin at each end. Plunge tomatoes into boiling water for 30 seconds, remove and set aside to cool. When cooled, peel skin.

Heat oil in a heavy 4–5 quart Dutch oven over medium high heat, add beef to pan in batches and cook until brow, stirring occasionally, for approximately 3 minutes per batch. Transfer browned beef to a bowl and set aside.

Add onions to same pan and cook until light brown, stirring frequently, approximately 5 minutes. Add tomatoes, garlic, herbs and cumin then stir in vegetable juice and bring to a boil.

Add back beef, cover and bake in oven until beef is tender, approximately 2 hours. Season with pepper and serve.

Serves 4

Stuffed Beef Tenderloin

1–3 to 4 pound beef tenderloin, center cut
1 10-ounce package frozen chopped spinach, thawed
8 ounces feta cheese, room temperature
1 tablespoon chopped fresh rosemary
1 tablespoon chopped fresh thyme
1 12-ounce jar roasted red peppers, drained
Freshly ground pepper
1 bunch fresh basil leaves
2 tablespoons coconut oil
2 shallots, minced
1 cup beef stock
1 tablespoon cornstarch dissolved in additional ¼ cup beef stock
5 tablespoons tomato paste
1 teaspoon fresh rosemary
2 tablespoons butter, cold, cut into pieces

Butterfly the beef tenderloin by cutting the beef lengthwise down the center about two-thirds of the way through. Open the beef tenderloin laying flat. Use a meat mallet, or small heavy bottomed pan, to pound the meat to ¾ inch thickness.

Place the spinach in a colander and squeeze out as much of the moisture as possible. Mix the spinach, feta cheese, fresh rosemary, and thyme in a large bowl.

Season flattened tenderloin with freshly ground pepper. Place the red peppers on top of the beef leaving a 1-inch border. Place the fresh basil leaves on top of the red peppers.

Spread the cheese mixture on one end over the peppers and basil. Roll the beef jellyroll style. Use butcher string or bamboo skewers to secure.

Refrigerate for at least one hour or until ready to cook and serve.

Preheat the oven to 375 degrees F.

Heat 2 tablespoons coconut oil in a large roasting pan over medium high heat. Brown beef tenderloin on all sides. Place on a rack in a roasting pan and roast for 30 to 40 minutes. Use a meat thermometer to determine doneness.

Cook the shallots over medium high heat in the pan used to brown the beef until just soft, add 1 cup beef stock and bring to a boil.

Stir in the dissolved cornstarch and cook, stirring until thickened. Add tomato paste and fresh rosemary, season with pepper.

Remove the tenderloin from pan and allow to rest, at least 10 minutes.

Remove the rack and place pan over medium high heat. Add ¼ cup of beef stock, stir to loosen bits and deglaze pan. Add the previously made sauce and simmer for 2 minutes. Reduce the heat, stir in the cold butter until just combined.

Cut the stuffed beef tenderloin into 1-inch slices. Pour the sauce onto a dinner plate. Place a slice of tenderloin on top and garnish with fresh basil leaves.

Beef Stroganoff

¾ pound beef tenderloin
1 tablespoon coconut oil
1 medium onion, chopped
2 cloves garlic, chopped
2 tablespoons cornstarch, dissolved in 2 tablespoons water
2 tablespoons tomato paste
1½ cups beef or vegetable stock
1 large green bell pepper, diced
4 tablespoons plain unsweetened yogurt
½ teaspoon nutmeg
Pepper to taste

Trim any excess fat from the beef and cut into ½ inch thick slices.

In a skillet heat the oil and fry the meat with the onions for 5 minutes until lightly browned. Stir in cornstarch, add tomato paste and pour in the stock, mixing thoroughly. Add bell pepper, nutmeg and pepper to taste.

Bring to a boil, reduce heat to a simmer and cook for 20 minutes, until the meat is tender and cooked.

Remove from heat and stir in yogurt just before serving.

Serves 4

Grilled Jamaican Jerk Chicken

6 chicken legs and thighs, attached
15 fresh chili peppers
2 tablespoons dried rosemary
2 tablespoons parsley, chopped
2 tablespoons dried basil
2 tablespoons dried thyme
2 tablespoons mustard seeds
4 tablespoons dry mustard
3 scallions, chopped fine
1 teaspoon black pepper
2 limes, juiced
¼ cup water

Preheat grill.

Combine the water and dry mustard powder, mix well and set aside. Combine the remaining ingredients in a food processor and blend, add in the mustard mixture and blend into a paste.

Rub the chicken pieces with the paste. Place over grill with very low heat; either push the coals to one side and place chicken on opposite side or only light one side of the gas grill. Cover and cook approximately 30 minutes. Check the chicken to see if the juices are running clear, if not cook another 10–15 minutes and check again.

Note: If you do not have a covered grill, cook the chicken about 1 hour. It is important to cook slowly over low heat to prevent burning of the paste rub.

Serves 4 to 6

Lamb and Peppers

12 ounces lean lamb, trimmed
2 medium red onions, sliced
1 large red bell pepper, thickly sliced
1 large green bell pepper, thickly sliced
1 large orange or yellow bell pepper, thickly sliced
1 lemon, juiced
1¼ cups vegetable stock
2 tablespoons coconut oil
Pinch of saffron strands
¾ cup chopped tomatoes
1 15-ounce can garbanzo beans, drained
1 teaspoon harissa sauce (see condiments section)
Salt and pepper to taste

Toss red onions in lemon juice and put into a saucepan with the bell peppers, cinnamon stick and saffron. Pour in vegetable stock and bring to a boil, reduce heat to a simmer, cover and cook for 5 minutes.

In a skillet, heat oil and brown the lamb for 3–4 minutes until well browned. Remove lamb and add to saucepan, season with pepper.

Stir in harissa sauce, tomatoes and beans. Mix well. Bring to a boil, reduce heat and simmer for 20 minutes.

Serves 4

RELISHES AND SAUCES

rel·ish: something adding a zestful flavor; a condiment eaten with other food to add flavor

sauce: something that adds zest or piquancy

Relishes and Sauces

Pico de Gallo Salsa

4 plum tomatoes, seeded and chopped
½ cup onion, finely chopped
2 fresh chili peppers, mild or hot, seeded and finely chopped
2 tablespoons chopped orange or yellow bell pepper
1½ teaspoon finely chopped fresh cilantro
1 teaspoon limejuice
Salt and pepper, to taste

Combine ingredients in a glass or other non-reactive bowl and refrigerate for at least 30 minutes before serving.

Makes approximately 2 cups

Vegetable Dipping Sauce

1 small lemon
1 tablespoon tomato, very finely chopped
1 teaspoon dry mustard
4 tablespoons plain unsweetened yogurt
2 fresh basil leaves
Salt and pepper to taste

Cut off the rind from ½ of the lemon and cut into thin julienne strips. Be sure you do not cut off the white pith, it is bitter.

In a bowl, combine the juice of the whole lemon and rind from the ½ lemon. Add the tomato, mustard and yogurt. Mix well and season with salt and pepper to taste.

Shred the basil leaves and mix into the dipping sauce.

Makes approximately 1½ cups

Curry Paste

6 dried hot red chilies, 1½ to 2 inches long
2 tablespoons minced shallots or scallions, white part only
1 tablespoon minced garlic
1 tablespoon paprika
2 tablespoons lemon grass, white part only (or very thin strips of lemon peel)
1 teaspoon ground ginger
1 teaspoon caraway seed
1 teaspoon coriander seed
1 teaspoon lemon rind, finely grated

Under cold running water, wash the chilies and remove their stems and seeds; break the pods into small pieces.

Combine the chilies, shallots (or scallions), garlic, paprika, lemon grass or lemon peel, ginger, caraway, and coriander in a blender and blend at high speed for 20 to 30 seconds.

Turn off the machine, scrape down the sides and blend again until the mixture is a smooth paste. The paste may be safely kept for a month or so when tightly covered and refrigerated.

Barbeque Sauce

1 cup catsup (see condiments for recipe)
1 cup water
¼ cup lemon juice
¾ teaspoon garlic powder
½ teaspoon onion powder
½ teaspoon dry mustard
⅜ teaspoon crushed stevia leaf powder
1 teaspoon celery seed
3 dashes hot pepper sauce

In a saucepan, combine catsup, water, lemon juice, stevia, hot pepper sauce, garlic and onion powder, dry mustard, and celery seed. Bring to boil, reduce heat and simmer, uncovered, for 30 minutes.

Makes 1½ cups

Garam Marsala

1 tablespoon cardamom seeds
2 inch stick cinnamon
1 teaspoon cumin seeds
1 teaspoon whole cloves
1 teaspoon black peppercorns
½ teaspoon grated nutmeg

Place all ingredients in a clean coffee grinder. Grind until all combined and a fine powder, about 45 seconds. This makes 3 tablespoons. Store in small jar away from heat or in freezer for up to a year.

Oyster Sauce

2 cups of fresh oyster meat
3 cups of water
1 cup of bottled clam juice
1 clove garlic, crushed
1 green onion, white portion only
1 slice of fresh ginger, ⅛ inch thick, peeled
¼ cup of Bragg's Amino Acids
⅜ teaspoon powdered stevia leaf powder
2 teaspoons cornstarch
3 tablespoons water

Wash and drain the oyster meat.

In a saucepan, bring the oyster meat, water, clam juice, salt, garlic, green onion and ginger to a boil. Reduce heat to a simmer, cover, and simmer for 30 minutes.

In a small bowl, mix the Braggs, stevia, cornstarch, and 3 tablespoons of water. Remove the lid from the saucepan and gradually add cornstarch mixture, while stirring. Simmer for another 10 minutes, stirring periodically, until thickened.

Set a strainer over a large bowl and strain the oyster mixture to remove solids, which you discard.

Cucumber Relish

3 medium cucumbers
½ medium onion
¼ cup lemon juice
⅜ teaspoon crushed stevia leaf powder
¼ teaspoon dried dill weed

Slice cucumbers in half lengthwise, scoop out seeds. Grind in a food processor along with onions until very fine, drain.

Stir in lemon juice, stevia and dried dill weed. Chill overnight.

Makes about 4 cups

Cucumber Raita

1 cucumber, peeled and seeded
2 cups plain unsweetened yogurt
1 teaspoon chili powder
Salt

Remove seeds from cucumber and grate. Sprinkle with salt and place in a strainer over a bowl and let stand 10 minutes to drain. Rinse off salt and squeeze out any additional moisture by pressing cucumber with the bottom of a glass. Mix the cucumber into the yogurt and stir in chili powder. Chill before serving

Dill Sauce

2 tablespoons butter
1 tablespoons cornstarch, dissolved in 2 tablespoons water
1 teaspoon instant chicken bouillon granules dissolved in 1 cup hot water
⅜ teaspoon crushed stevia leaf powder
1 teaspoon dried dill weed
1 teaspoon lemon juice

In a saucepan melt butter and stir in cornstarch. Add bouillon and water to cornstarch mixture. Stir in stevia, dill weed and lemon juice and cook and stir until thickened.

Harissa Sauce

10 dried red New Mexico chilies, stems and seeds removed
2 tablespoons extra virgin or cold pressed olive oil
5 cloves of garlic
1 teaspoon cumin
1 teaspoon cinnamon
1 teaspoon ground coriander
1 teaspoon caraway seeds

Cover chilies with hot water and let stand for 15 minutes until soft. Place all ingredients in a blender and puree until smooth. Use chili water to thin, if needed.

Cover with a thin film of olive oil to preserve. This will keep 2 months in the refrigerator.

Red Pepper Chutney

3 red bell peppers
2 green onions
2 tablespoons cold pressed or extra virgin olive oil
⅛ teaspoon cumin seeds
⅛ teaspoon caraway seeds
⅛ teaspoon coriander seeds
1 tablespoon minced fresh cilantro

1 tablespoon lime juice
Freshly ground black pepper
Cayenne pepper to taste

Preheat grill or broiler.

Coat the red peppers and green onions lightly with the olive oil and place over grill or under hot broiler. Cook, turning frequently, to blacken. Remove the green onions as soon as they turn bright green and the outer leaves just blackened. The skin on the peppers should blacken thoroughly and blister.

After peppers are charred, remove and place them in a bowl of ice water. Remove the skin and seeds from the peppers under water. Cut the green onions into 1-inch lengths and chop the peppers roughly.

Place a small skillet over medium heat. Add the cumin, coriander, and caraway and toast until the spices begin to give off a nutty aroma, about 1 to 2 minutes. Remove from heat and let the spices cool.

Transfer spice mix to a food processor or spice grinder and grind into a fine powder. Add to the pepper and onion mixture. Stir in cilantro, lime juice, pepper, and cayenne. Check for seasoning and adjust, add salt if necessary.

Lemon Chutney

1 tablespoon safflower oil
1 small whole chili, fresh or dried, chopped or crumbled
½ teaspoon cumin seed
¼ teaspoon nutmeg
¼ teaspoon mustard seed
4 large tomatoes, very thinly sliced
½ fresh lemon
⅓ cup golden raisins
1 tablespoon crushed stevia leaf powder

Heat oil in a saucepan, add chili, cumin, nutmeg and mustard seed. When the seeds start to jump in the oil, add the tomatoes.

Quarter the lemon and remove seeds, layer with the spices in pan. Simmer, stirring to keep from sticking, for 15 minutes.

Stir in the raisins and the stevia. Continue to simmer, stirring frequently, until the mixture thickens, about 30 minutes.

Cool and store chutney in the refrigerator.

Makes approximately 2 cups

SALADS AND SALAD DRESSINGS

sal·ad: green vegetables (as lettuce, endive, or romaine) and often tomatoes, cucumbers, or radishes served with dressing

sal·ad dress·ing: a dressing either uncooked or cooked that is used for salad

Salads and Salad Dressings

Chinese Chicken Salad

4 chicken breasts, cooked and cut into pieces
3 celery stalks, chopped
1 cup bean sprouts
1 small can sliced water chestnuts, drained
1 carrot cut in thin strips
2 tablespoons Bragg's amino acids
¼ teaspoon onion powder
¼ teaspoon ground ginger
¼ teaspoon dry mustard
¼ teaspoon pepper
4 large leaves Boston or Romaine lettuce
6 whole black pitted olives

In a small bowl mix Braggs, onion powder, ginger and dry mustard with pepper and set aside. Combine the vegetables in another bowl and sprinkle with the liquid and toss. Fill lettuce leaves with mixture.

Serves 4

Curried Crab Salad

12 ounces crabmeat
1 teaspoon curry powder
1 tablespoon mayonnaise (see condiments)
2 tablespoons plain unsweetened yogurt
2 tablespoons cilantro, chopped
4 leaves Bib or Boston lettuce, washed and dried

Mix together curry, mayonnaise, yogurt and cilantro, add crabmeat and toss to coat. Chill.

Serve in lettuce cups.

Serves 4

Asian Bok Choy Salad

½ cup water
1½ teaspoons stevia crushed leaf powder
1 lemon, juiced
2 tablespoons Bragg's amino acids
⅓ cup olive oil
2 medium heads bok choy, torn
4 green onions, chopped
1 cup pine nuts

Combine water, stevia, lemon juice, and Braggs with olive oil and refrigerate. In a medium bowl, toss bok choy and green onions with pine nuts. Sprinkle with chilled dressing.

Serves 4

Wilted Spinach Salad

8 cups fresh spinach, torn
¼ cup sliced green onion
3 slices crisp cooked uncured pancetta, reserve drippings
2 teaspoons lemon juice
Pinch of crushed stevia leaf powder
1 hard boiled organic egg, chopped

In a large skillet with the pancetta drippings stir in lemon juice and stevia. Remove from heat, add in spinach and green onion and toss to coat well.

Place in serving bowl and sprinkle with chopped egg and crumbled bacon, serve warm

Serves 6

Black Bean and Millet Salad

1 cup millet, uncooked
3 cups water

1½ cups canned black beans
2 large tomatoes, chopped
1 medium onion, chopped
1 medium cucumber

For dressing:
⅓ cup water
3 tablespoons lemon juice
2 teaspoons Bragg's amino acids
1 teaspoon garlic, minced
¼ teaspoon allspice
¼ teaspoon black pepper
½ teaspoon cumin

Cook the millet in water until all the water is absorbed, approximately 30–45 minutes. Fluff with a fork and allow to cool slightly.

Mix dressing until well blended. Cover and refrigerate until very chilled.

In a very large bowl, combine millet, black beans, tomatoes, and onion. Peel alternate strips of cucumber, leaving strips of peel between and quarter lengthwise. Remove the seeds and cut into ½ inch slices. Add to the salad.

Pour dressing over salad and toss to blend.

Serves 4

Asparagus Beet Salad

1 pound fresh asparagus, cut into 2 inch pieces
½ cup extra virgin or cold pressed olive oil
¼ cup finely chopped canned beets
2 tablespoons lemon juice
¼ teaspoon crushed stevia leaf powder
1 teaspoon paprika
½ teaspoon dry mustard
4 drops hot sauce

5 cups mixed lettuces
1 hard boiled organic egg, chopped
¼ cup sliced green onion

In a saucepan place the asparagus with water 1 inch above level of asparagus, boil for 8 to 10 minutes or until tender. Drain and chill.

Combine oil, beets, lemon juice, and stevia, with the paprika, dry mustard and hot sauce. Mix well and chill.

In a large bowl, combine chilled asparagus, lettuce, chopped egg, and green onion. Pour dressing over salad and toss gently. Add beets and serve.

Serves 6

Greek Salad

10-ounces cooked lamb or beef cut into julienne strips
6 cups curly endive, torn
3 cups romaine lettuce, torn
2 tomatoes, peeled and chopped
¾ cup fresh feta cheese
¼ cup sliced black olives
¼ cup sliced green onion
⅔ cup extra virgin or cold pressed olive oil
⅓ cup lemon juice
¼ teaspoon dried oregano, crushed
1 2-ounce can anchovy filets, drained (optional)
⅛ teaspoon pepper

In a mixing bowl, toss lettuces with lamb, tomatoes, feta, olives and onion.

In a separate bowl combine oil, lemon juice, oregano and pepper. Mix well, and pour over the salad mixture and toss lightly.

Serves 6

Gazpacho Tomato Salad

3 medium tomatoes, cut into eight pieces
1 medium cucumber, thinly sliced
1 medium green bell pepper, chopped
2 small onions, sliced and separated into rings
3 tablespoons chopped parsley
¼ cup extra virgin or cold pressed olive oil
1 teaspoon dried basil, crushed
1 clove garlic, minced
3 drops of hot pepper sauce

In a bowl combine oil, lemon juice, hot sauce, garlic and basil; mix well. Add in vegetables and toss well to coat. Cover and chill 2–3 hours stirring occasionally.

Serves 4 to 6

Crunchy Coleslaw

⅔ cup mayonnaise (see condiments)
⅔ cup plain unsweetened yogurt
1 medium head cabbage, shredded
4 carrots
1 green bell pepper
2 tablespoons sunflower seeds
Dash Tabasco sauce
Pepper

In a bowl, combine yogurt, mayonnaise, Tabasco, and pepper to taste. Chill in refrigerator.

Wash shredded cabbage, drain and dry thoroughly. Peel carrot; place in a food processor and shred. Cut bell pepper in thin strips.

In a bowl combine vegetables, pour over dressing and toss well to mix. Scatter sunflower seeds over top.

Serves 10–12

Black Bean Salad

1 15-ounce can black beans, drained and rinsed
2 medium red bell peppers, chopped
2 tablespoons finely chopped sweet Vidalia onion
2 to 3 green onions, sliced
¼ teaspoon onion powder
¼ teaspoon dried leaf oregano
Dash garlic powder
Dash ground cayenne pepper, or to taste

For dressing:
2 tablespoons extra virgin or cold pressed olive oil
2 tablespoons lemon juice
¼ teaspoon onion powder
2 tablespoons chopped parsley

In blender or food processor, mix oil, lemon and onion powder. Stir in parsley.

In serving bowl, add beans, vegetables with onion, garlic powder and oregano. Pour dressing over vegetable mixture; toss well.

Serves 6

Spanish Salad

1 pound, ground pork
½ cup chopped onion
1 clove of garlic, minced
1 8-ounce can tomato sauce
1 7½-ounce can tomatoes, cut up
1 4-ounce can green chili peppers, rinsed, seeded and chopped
2 teaspoons chili powder
6 cups torn romaine lettuce
1 15-ounce can garbanzo beans, drained
½ cup sliced black olives
1 cup shredded Mozzarella cheese
1 cup cherry tomatoes, halved

1 medium green bell pepper, sliced lengthwise
1 large avocado, peeled and sliced

In a large skillet cook the pork with onions and garlic until browned and onion is tender. Stir in tomato sauce, tomatoes with juice from can, chili peppers and chili powder. Cook, stirring until thickened.

In a bowl, combine lettuce, beans, and olives. Place on serving plates and top with meat mixture and sprinkle with cheese and top with cherry tomato halves. Arrange avocado and bell pepper slices around sides.

Serves 6

Crab Salad

1 head of Boston lettuce
14-ounces crab meat, chilled and drained
2 large tomatoes cut in wedges
2 hard-boiled organic eggs cut in wedges
Paprika
1 lemon cut in wedges
1 cup mayonnaise (see condiments section)
¼ cup chili sauce (see condiments section)
¼ cup finely chopped green bell pepper
¼ cup finely chopped green onion
1 teaspoon lemon juice

In a bowl, combine mayonnaise, chili sauce, onion, bell pepper, green onion and lemon juice. Mix well, cover and chill.

Place 4 leaves of Boston lettuce on a plate.

Tear remaining lettuce in into pieces and place on the leaf cups. Break or chop crab into bite-size pieces and place on lettuce surround with tomato and egg wedges.

Pour dressing and sprinkle with paprika.

Serves 4

Black Eye Pea Salad

2 15-ounce cans black-eyed peas
½ cup finely chopped onion
½ cup finely chopped celery
1 small sweet red bell pepper, seeded and finely chopped

For dressing
¼ cup lemon juice
3 tablespoons chopped fresh basil, or 1 teaspoon dried
2 to 3 medium cloves garlic, crushed
¼ teaspoon crushed stevia leaf powder
¼ teaspoon freshly ground black pepper
1 cup olive oil
Fresh basil or parsley for garnish

In a serving bowl, combine black-eyed peas, onion, celery, and green pepper. Set aside.

In a small bowl whisk together the lemon juice, basil, garlic, stevia and pepper. Gradually whisk in the oil until the dressing is well blended.

Pour over pea mixture, cover and refrigerate until thoroughly chilled or overnight.

Serves 6

Root Salad

¾ cup carrots, shredded
1 cup daikon radish, shredded
½ cup red radishes, thinly sliced
¾ cup celery root, grated
2 celery stalks with leaves
2 tablespoons lime juice
½ teaspoon grated lime rind
1 teaspoon celery seeds
1 teaspoon dry mustard dissolved in 1 teaspoon water

1 tablespoon walnut oil
Chopped walnuts
Spring mix salad greens

On serving plates, place salad mix with a small mound of daikon, carrots and red radishes on top. Remove celery leaves and chop, set aside. Chop celery stalks finely and combine with 1-tablespoon lime juice. Place on top of mix on salad.

In a small bowl mix walnut oil, 1-tablespoon lime juice, mustard, lime rind, celery seeds and pepper to taste. Drizzle over salad and sprinkle chopped celery leaves over top.

Serves 4

Warm Lamb Salad

¼ cup olive oil
1½ pounds lamb steaks, 1 inch thick
1 small onion, minced
2 garlic cloves, crushed
1 cup chicken broth or stock
1 tablespoon fresh lemon juice
⅜ teaspoon crushed stevia leaf powder
½ teaspoon pepper
1 teaspoon dried dill weed
1 teaspoon dried oregano
2 green bell peppers, sliced
⅓ cup chopped parsley
2 cups (8 ounces) crumbled feta cheese
Yogurt dressing (see below)
Mixed lettuces

In a heavy pan, heat oil and sauté steaks, browning on both sides. Set aside to rest 10 minutes.

To the same pan add onion and garlic and sauté 2 minutes. Cut steaks into 2-inch slices, return to pan and add broth, lemon juice, sugar, stevia, pepper, dill, and oregano. Stir well. Cover and cook 15 minutes.

Add bell pepper and cook 2 minutes more. Add the cooked mixture to a bowl, add parsley and cheese and toss. Arrange lettuce on a serving platter and top with lamb mixture. Serve with yogurt dressing.

Serves 6

Yogurt Dressing

¼ cup extra virgin or cold-pressed olive oil
¼ cup plain unsweetened yogurt
1 tablespoon fresh lemon juice
1 garlic clove, crushed
½ teaspoon dried dill weed

Combine oil, yogurt, lemon juice, garlic and dill in a blender or food processor and mix until thoroughly blended. Store in refrigerator.

Makes 6 servings

Creamy Onion Dill Dressing

6 ounces silken tofu
2 teaspoons lemon juice
1 tablespoon dried minced onion
1 teaspoon fresh dill

Place all ingredients in a food processor and blend until smooth.

Makes approximately ½ cup

Green Goddess Dressing

½ cup mayonnaise (see condiments)
¼ cup green onions, chopped
2 tablespoons chives, chopped
2 tablespoons flat leaf parsley, chopped
1 tablespoon anchovy paste

1 tablespoon fresh lemon juice
¼ teaspoon salt
⅛ teaspoon fresh cracked black pepper

Combine all ingredients in a food processor or blender and blend until creamy.

Makes approx ½ cup

Tahini Salad Dressing

⅔ cup extra virgin or cold pressed olive oil
⅓ cup fresh lemon juice
⅓ cup tahini
¼ cup Braggs amino acids
⅜ teaspoon crushed stevia leaf powder
½ teaspoon dried oregano
1 tablespoon mayonnaise (see condiments)
Pepper to taste

Combine all ingredients in a blender and process until smooth.

Lemon Tamari Salad Dressing

1 cup olive oil
⅓ cup fresh lemon juice
½ cup sesame tahini
3 tablespoons Braggs amino acids
¼ medium onion, minced
¼ medium bell pepper, minced
⅔ stalk celery, minced
1 teaspoon black pepper

Puree all ingredients in a food processor.

Makes 1¾ cups

Parsley Dressing

2 tablespoons extra virgin or cold pressed olive oil
2 tablespoons lemon juice
¼ teaspoon onion powder
2 tablespoons chopped parsley

In blender, mix oil, lemon and onion powder. Stir in parsley and serve

Makes a single serving

Sweet Mustard Dressing

1 cup extra virgin or cold pressed olive oil
1 teaspoon dry mustard
¾ teaspoon crushed stevia leaf powder
⅛ teaspoon garlic powder
Pinch of white pepper

Combine all ingredients in a food processor or blender and blend until combined.

Makes approximately 1 cup

Mustard Basil Dressing

¼ cup extra virgin or cold pressed olive oil
2 tablespoons minced fresh basil
1 clove garlic, diced
¼ teaspoon dry mustard
¼ teaspoon oregano
1 teaspoon fresh squeezed lemon juice
Pepper to taste

Combine all ingredients in a blender and mix to combine.

Makes approximately ¼ cup

Russian Salad Dressing

1 cup vegetable juice
½ cup extra virgin or cold pressed olive oil
½ cup lemon juice
⅜ teaspoon crushed stevia leaf powder
1 teaspoon paprika
1 teaspoon onion powder
1 teaspoon garlic powder

Process or blend until well mixed.

Makes approximately 2 cups

Tomato Dressing

⅓ cup tomato puree
½ cup extra virgin or cold pressed olive oil
⅓ cup lemon juice
1 clove garlic
1 small onion, chopped
⅜ teaspoon crushed stevia leaf powder

Mix up in a blender of food processor until smooth.

Makes approximately ¾ cup

Creamy Caesar Dressing

1 raw or coddled organic egg
3 tablespoons lemon juice
2 garlic cloves
1 cup extra virgin or cold pressed olive oil
1 2-ounce tin of anchovies in olive oil (optional)

Blend egg, lemon juice, anchovies and garlic in food processor and slowly drizzle in the olive oil, blending until thickened and creamy.

Makes approximately 1 cup

Ginger Salad Dressing

6–7 baby carrots
1 stalk celery
1 teaspoon Braggs amino acids
1 tablespoon cold pressed or extra virgin olive oil
1 tablespoon ground ginger root
Juice of ½ lemon
½ clove of garlic

Combine all ingredients in a food processor or blender until well blended.

Makes approximately ¼ cup

Creamy Sesame Garlic Dressing

2 cloves garlic, crushed
3 tablespoons tahini
½ cup plain almond milk
2 tablespoons fresh-squeezed lemon juice
1 teaspoon toasted sesame oil

Process all ingredients in a blender until smooth.

Makes approximately ½ cup

Pomegranate Basil Vinaigrette

½ cup extra virgin olive oil
¼ cup unsweetened pomegranate juice
1 teaspoon lemon juice
6–8 fresh basil leaves, minced

¼–½ teaspoon dry mustard powder
1 clove garlic, crushed

Process all ingredients in a blender or food processor until smooth.

Cilantro Lime Yogurt Dressing

1 cup plain unsweetened yogurt
1 tablespoon minced fresh cilantro
1 tablespoon minced green onion
2 teaspoons fresh lime juice

In a small bowl, combine the yogurt, cilantro, scallions, and limejuice. Set aside for at least an hour to allow flavors to meld.

Tsatsiki

4–5 cloves garlic crushed, juices saved with the garlic
1 cup plain unsweetened yogurt
½ tablespoon olive oil
Pepper
¼ cucumber, peeled, grated, and drained

Combine crushed garlic and juices with yogurt, olive oil and add pepper to taste.

Refrigerate at least ½ hour, mix in cucumber right before serving

Greek Dressing Number One

1 tablespoon oregano
1 teaspoon parsley
5 tablespoons extra virgin or cold-pressed olive oil
2 to 3 teaspoons lemon juice
Garlic powder
Pepper to taste

Combine all ingredients and mix well.

Greek Dressing Number Two

¼ cup safflower oil
⅛ teaspoon crushed stevia leaf powder
⅛ teaspoon oregano
¼ cup lemon juice
⅛ teaspoon dry mustard

Combine all ingredients and mix well.

Moroccan Spice Dressing

½ teaspoon dry mustard
½ teaspoon crushed stevia leaf powder
¼ teaspoon curry powder or to taste
½ teaspoon paprika
2 teaspoons extra virgin or cold-pressed olive oil
2 teaspoons lemon or lime juice

Put all ingredients in a food processor or blender and mix well.

VEGETABLES AND SIDE DISHES

veg·e·ta·ble: a usually herbaceous plant (as the cabbage, bean, or potato) grown for an edible part that is usually eaten as part of a meal

side dish: a food served separately along with the main course

Side Dishes and Vegetables

Millet Pilaf

1 cup shelled millet seed
1 medium onion chopped
Dash freshly ground pepper
½ stick butter
3 cups water
3 chicken or beef bullion cubes

Put millet into a dry heavy skillet, with a cover. Over medium heat, cook millet, stirring constantly for 2 to 3 minutes or until golden brown. Add remaining ingredients; millet will sizzle.

Simmer tightly covered, over low heat for 15 to 20 minutes or until liquid is absorbed.

Stir occasionally, and if necessary add more boiling water to prevent sticking. Serve hot.

Herbed Wild Rice

2 cups wild rice
3 tablespoons extra-virgin olive oil
¼ cup chopped fresh flat-leaf parsley
¼ cup chopped fresh marjoram
Freshly ground pepper

Rinse wild rice well under cold running water. Drain well, and set aside.

Bring a large saucepan of water to a boil. Stir in wild rice, reduce to a simmer, and cook until wild rice is tender, about 40 minutes.

In a bowl mix and stir in oil with rice, parsley, and marjoram. Season with pepper and serve at room temperature or chilled.

Serves 4

Rice Salad

1 cup uncooked wild rice
2 6-ounce jars marinated artichoke heart quarters, one drained/one undrained
3 medium tomatoes, chopped
1 8-ounce can sliced water chestnuts, drained
1 cup dressing

    For dressing:
    1 raw or coddled organic egg
    3 tablespoons lemon juice
    2 garlic cloves
    1 cup extra virgin or cold pressed olive oil
    1 2-ounce tin of anchovies in olive oil (optional)

Rinse wild rice thoroughly. In a large saucepan, add rice to 3 ½-cups water. Bring to a boil; stir, then reduce heat and simmer, covered for 40–45 minutes just until kernels open.

Make dressing by combining egg, lemon juice and garlic in a food processor and drizzle in olive oil slowly while you blend until thickened and creamy. Fluff rice with fork and set aside to cool.

To rice add artichoke hearts, chopped tomatoes, and water chestnuts. Pour over dressing and toss gently.

Cover and chill at least 8 hours. Drain before serving. You can also elect to serve the salad right away without draining.

Makes 8 to 10 servings

Broiled Vegetable Skewers

4 baby eggplant
1 large zucchini
2 medium red onions
1 red bell pepper
1 green bell pepper

1 orange or yellow bell pepper
1 tablespoon extra virgin or cold pressed olive oil
1 clove garlic, crushed
1 tablespoon fresh rosemary, chopped
Freshly ground pepper

Preheat broiler. Soak skewers in water.

Clean and cut bell peppers into uniform 1-inch pieces. Cut zucchini in half and slice into ½ inch thick pieces. Trim tops off eggplant and cut into quarters lengthwise. Cut onions into 8 even-size wedges.

Mix, in a small bowl, the lemon juice, olive oil, garlic, rosemary and pepper to taste. Pour over vegetables and toss well to coat. Place pieces, alternately, onto soaked skewers.

Broil, turning frequently, until vegetables begin to char and cooked, approximately 10 minutes.

Serves 8

"Mashed" Potatoes

6 cups chopped cauliflower
¼ cup flax oil
Spike All Purpose Seasoning to taste

Process cauliflower in a food processor and chop until grainy. In a large pot on low temperature, add oil, spices and cauliflower, stirring to coat and heat thoroughly.

Quinoa Tabooleh

2 cups quinoa, cooked
½ teaspoon basil
1 cup chopped parsley
½ cup lemon juice
½ cup chopped scallions
½ cup cold pressed or extra virgin olive oil

2 tablespoons fresh mint
Freshly ground pepper
1 teaspoon dried mint
Whole lettuce leaves
1 clove of garlic, pressed
¼ cup black olives, sliced

In a mixing bowl combine quinoa, basil, parsley, lemon juice, scallions, olive oil, fresh and dried mint, garlic and pepper; toss together lightly. Chill for 1 hour or more to allow flavors to blend.

Wash and dry lettuce leaves and line a salad bowl. Add tabooleh and garnish with olives.

Serves 4

Garlic Tomatoes with Quinoa

1 cup quinoa
1 tablespoon butter
8 sun-dried tomatoes (not oil-packed), diced
2 shallots, minced
1 clove garlic, minced
2 cups vegetable stock
Pinch of cayenne pepper
2 tablespoon chopped fresh parsley
Freshly ground black pepper

Place quinoa in a fine-meshed sieve and rinse under warm running water for 1 minute, set aside.

Heat butter in a heavy, medium saucepan over medium heat. Add tomatoes, shallots, garlic and sauté for 3–5 minutes, or until shallots are softened.

Add stock and bring to a boil. Stir in quinoa and cayenne, return to boil, then reduce heat to low and simmer covered, for about 30 minutes, or until liquid is absorbed.

Let sit for 5 minutes, and fluff with a fork to separate. Stir in fresh parsley and season with pepper.

Serves 4

Rutabaga Casserole

4 cups cooked, mashed rutabaga
4 tablespoons melted butter
1 teaspoon fresh chopped dill weed or ½ teaspoon dried
Dash of pepper and paprika
4 organic eggs, separated

Preheat oven to 375 degrees F.

Combine mashed rutabaga, butter, dill, pepper, and paprika. Blend in egg yolks.

Beat egg whites until stiff peaks form; fold into the rutabaga mixture. Lightly pile into a greased 1½-quart casserole.

Bake for 30 to 40 minutes, until set and top is golden brown.

Serves 4 to 6

Quinoa and Vegetables

3 cups cooked quinoa (can be cooked in water or broth)
2 tablespoons cold pressed or extra virgin olive oil
1½ inch piece fresh ginger, peeled and minced
1 small carrot, peeled and diced
1 celery stalk, diced
½ red bell pepper, seeded and finely diced
½ green bell pepper, seeded and finely diced
2 scallions, white part only, finely sliced
Freshly ground black pepper
¼ cup fresh flat-leaf parsley, chopped or 1-tablespoon fresh thyme leaves

In a large skillet over medium-high heat, heat oil with ginger. When oil is hot and ginger smells aromatic, but not yet colored—approximately 2 minutes—add carrot and sauté 1 minute.

Stir in celery; add red and green peppers and scallions. Sauté to heat veggies through. Stir in hot quinoa and season with pepper. Stir in parsley or thyme leaves and serve immediately.

Serves 4

Mashed Rutabagas

4 large rutabagas
Water
1 tablespoon extra virgin or cold pressed olive oil
Dash of nutmeg
Fresh ground pepper to taste

Peel rutabagas and cut into chunks. In a 4-quart saucepan, add rutabagas and 2 inches of water. Cover saucepan, and bring to a boil over high heat.

Turn heat down to medium and cook about 12–15 minutes or until fork tender. Drain, reserving cooking liquid. Using a potato masher, coarsely mash rutabagas in the saucepan, adding cooking liquid as needed for moisture.

Add olive oil and season to taste with pepper and sprinkle with dash of nutmeg.

Serves 6

Dilled Zucchini

1 pound zucchini
2 tablespoons butter
1 tablespoon parsley
¼ teaspoon dried dill weed
Dash of pepper

Slice squash and place in a skillet with melted butter, parsley, dill and pepper.

Cover and cook 8 to 10 minutes, stirring often.

Serves 3 to 4

Herbed Mixed Vegetables

1 head of cauliflower broken into 4 equal pieces
1 cup of broccoli florets
8 tablespoons extra virgin or cold pressed olive oil
4 tablespoons butter
5 tablespoons cilantro, chopped
2 teaspoons ginger, peeled and grated
2 lemons, juiced and grated rinds
⅓ cup shredded mozzarella

Preheat broiler.

Bring to boil water in a saucepan and cook cauliflower and broccoli until crisp tender, approximately 10 minutes.

Meanwhile heat the butter and oil in a skillet. Add ginger, lemon juice, rind, and cilantro. Simmer for 2–3 minutes, season with pepper to taste. Add cauliflower, broccoli and toss.

Place mixture in an ovenproof dish and sprinkle cheese on top. Place under broiler and melt cheese until bubbly.

Serves 4

Almond Green Beans

1 pound green beans, washed and cleaned
2 tablespoons slivered almonds
2 tablespoons butter
1 teaspoon lemon juice

Steam beans until tender but still firm, approx 12 to 20 minutes, drain.

While beans are cooking, sauté almonds in a skillet with the butter over low heat, stirring, until golden. Remove from heat and add lemon juice, add drained beans, toss and serve.

Serves 6

Lemony Artichokes

1 quart cold water
¼ cup plus 1 tablespoon lemon juice
8 baby artichokes
4 teaspoons extra virgin or cold pressed olive oil
2 teaspoons unsalted butter
4 cloves garlic, minced
¾ cup chicken stock or water
Freshly ground pepper
2 teaspoons finely chopped fresh oregano leaves
2 ounces feta cheese, crumbled, approximately ⅓ cup

In a large non-reactive bowl, combine the water and ¼ cup of the lemon juice.

Cut ½ inch off the top of artichokes, cut off the stem. Peel and discard most of the outer leaves until you reach the tender, light green inner leaves. Cut artichokes in quarters lengthwise and remove choke. Put in the bowl of lemon water and toss. Set aside.

In a large pan, heat the olive oil and butter over medium heat. Add the minced garlic and cook for 1 minute. Remove the artichokes from the water, dry and add to the pan. Sauté while stirring frequently until edges of artichokes brown and become caramelized; approximately 6 to 8 minutes.

Add ½ cup of the chicken stock, cover and cook, stirring occasionally, until tender but still firm, approximately 10 minutes. If pan is drying or begins to burn add a tablespoon or two of stock or water.

Remove cover and turn the heat to high. Add remaining ¼-cup chicken stock and bring to a boil. Reduce the liquid to 1 tablespoon and lower heat to medium; add 1 tablespoon lemon juice, pepper to taste, and the oregano. Stir well.

Place artichokes on a serving platter and top with cheese.

Serves 4

Eggplant Patties

1 large eggplant, sliced in rounds
1 cup grated mozzarella cheese
2 sun-dried tomatoes, chopped
1 tablespoon lemon juice
3 tablespoons extra virgin or cold pressed olive oil
Freshly ground pepper

Preheat broiler.

In a small bowl, mix lemon juice and oil until well blended, season with pepper to taste. Brush eggplant with mixture and place under broiler 2–3 minutes, without turning.

Turn over half of eggplant slices, sprinkle with cheese and chopped sun-dried tomatoes. Place other half of slices on top with palest side up. Broil another 1–2 minutes, turn over, baste with oil mix and broil other side.

Serves 2–4

Zucchini Cakes

2 cups coarsely grated zucchini
½ cup soy flour
1 teaspoon non-aluminum baking powder
1 small onion, finely chopped
1 organic egg, beaten

Mix the flour with the baking powder. Sprinkle the flour mixture over the zucchini and onions and mix well. Add egg and mix again.

Fry cakes of about one tablespoon of batter in a buttered or oiled skillet.

Buckwheat and Spinach

1 large Spanish onion
2 cloves of garlic
2 cups buckwheat
1 teaspoon fresh ground black pepper
2 cups vegetable stock
1 pound spinach
1 tablespoon butter
1 teaspoon extra virgin or cold pressed olive oil

Cook the buckwheat with the pepper to taste in the vegetable stock until tender.

Meanwhile, in a small skillet, cook the onion and garlic in the butter and olive oil. Finely chop the spinach and add it with the cooked and drained buckwheat to the skillet. Simmer about 15 minutes.

Serves 4

Stuffed Green Peppers

1 tablespoon butter
4 green bell peppers
1½ pounds ground sirloin
½ pound ground sausage
1 small white onion, diced fine
Oregano, seasoned pepper and fennel seed to taste, optional
6 Roma tomatoes, chopped
2 teaspoons of crushed garlic
6 ounces of fresh feta cheese, crumbled
½ cup shredded mozzarella cheese

Preheat oven to 350 degrees F. Oil a casserole dish.

Cook ground sirloin and sausage at medium heat, stirring often. When cooked through, drain thoroughly.

To a skillet, add butter, onions, garlic, oregano, seasoned pepper, fennel seed and 4 of the tomatoes. Simmer over low heat approximately 20 minutes.

Cut off stem tops, remove seeds and membranes from bell peppers; wash and dry thoroughly.

Fill all peppers with meat mixture half full, layer with feta and mozzarella cheese and more meat mixture.

Place peppers into a casserole dish and add the remaining chopped tomatoes to the dish along with any remaining meat mixture around the peppers. Sprinkle remaining feta and mozzarella cheese on top.

Bake for approximately 30 minutes or until browned and bubbly.

Serves 4

Roasted Veggies

1 medium zucchini, cut into bite-size pieces
1 medium yellow summer squash, cut into bite-size pieces
1 medium red bell pepper, cut into bite-size pieces
1 medium yellow bell pepper, cut into bite-size pieces
1 pound fresh asparagus, cut into bite-size pieces
1 red onion, chopped
3 tablespoons extra virgin or cold pressed olive oil
½ teaspoon black pepper

Preheat the oven to 450 degrees F

Place the zucchini, squash, bell peppers, asparagus, and red onion in a large roasting pan, and toss with the olive oil and black pepper. Spread in a single layer.

Roast for 30 minutes, stirring occasionally, until the vegetables are lightly browned and tender.

Serves 4

Broccoli Lemon Garlic

1 bunch broccoli, approximately 1 pound
¼ cup extra virgin or cold pressed olive oil
3 garlic cloves, diced
⅛ teaspoon freshly ground pepper
3 tablespoons fresh lemon juice

Steam broccoli approximately 5–6 minutes, or until tender but still crisp.

Meantime in a small frying pan, heat olive oil over low heat. Stir in garlic and cook slowly until golden brown, do not burn, approximately 1–2 minutes. Add pepper and lemon juice then pour over broccoli.

Serves 2–4

Spicy Mixed Veggies

½ cauliflower, in small florets
4 medium carrots peeled and sliced into ¼ inch rounds
2 medium turnips, peeled and cut in ½ inch chunks
3 green chilies, finely chopped
1¼ cups coconut oil
1 pound onions, finely chopped
3 medium tomatoes, chopped
½ red bell pepper, sliced
½ green bell pepper, sliced
1 teaspoon mustard seeds
1 teaspoon onion seeds
½ teaspoon white cumin seeds
3–4 curry leaves, chopped
1 tablespoon lemon juice
1 teaspoon chili powder

1 teaspoon garlic, crushed
1 teaspoon ginger root, finely chopped
¼ teaspoon turmeric
2 cups water
10 Cilantro leaves

In a large saucepan heat the oil; add mustard, onion and cumin seeds with curry leaves and fry until they turn a dark color. Add onions and cook over medium heat until golden brown.

Add tomatoes and bell peppers to saucepan and cook 5 minutes. Stir in garlic, ginger, chili powder, and turmeric. Add 1 ¼ cups of water; cover and simmer for 12 minutes

Serves 4

Herb Stuffed Tomatoes

5 beefsteak tomatoes
1 cup flat-leaf parsley, chopped
1 cup grated mozzarella cheese
¼ teaspoon freshly ground black pepper
1 teaspoon butter, softened
2 tablespoons extra virgin or cold pressed olive oil

Preheat oven to 375 degree F.

Cut tomatoes in half and hollow out the inside, discard the seeds and save the pulp. Be careful not to puncture the outside shell. Chop the pulp and put in a medium bowl, with parsley and cheese, season with pepper and mix to combine.

Fill the tomato halves with the mixture and place in a buttered baking dish. Drizzle olive oil over the top and bake until tops browned, approximately 20 minutes.

Serves 5–10

Sesame Asparagus

1 bunch fresh asparagus
2 tablespoons butter
1 teaspoon lemon juice
1 teaspoon toasted sesame seeds

Prepare asparagus by holding one spear lightly at the tip and end in two fingers and bend the stalk until it snaps. Use this piece to cut the asparagus to length. Lightly peel the bottom 1 inch of stalks.

Place asparagus in a steamer over boiling water and steam until tender crisp, approx 10 to 15 minutes. Immediately drain and plunge into a bowl of ice water and remove. This stops the cooking.

In skillet melt butter, add the asparagus and toss to heat through. Remove from heat, add in lemon juice and sesame, and toss well.

Serves 6

Baked Italian Green Beans

1 pound of fresh green beans, cooked
1 8-ounce can tomato sauce
1 tablespoon dry mustard mixed with 1 tablespoon water
2 teaspoons minced dried onion
⅛ teaspoon garlic powder
⅛ teaspoon pepper
½ cup shredded mozzarella cheese

Preheat oven to 350 degrees F.

Steam green beans until tender crisp, drain. Combine in a saucepan beans, tomato sauce, dried onion, garlic powder and pepper.

Place in a casserole dish, cover and bake for 20 minutes. Remove from oven, sprinkle with cheese and bake uncovered 1 to 2 minutes more to brown cheese.

Serves 6

Beets

4 medium beets, peeled
2¾ teaspoons crushed stevia leaf powder
2 tablespoons cornstarch
2 tablespoons lemon juice
1 tablespoon butter

Cut beets into ½ inch cubes and cook in boiling water for 30 to 35 minutes. Drain and reserve ⅓ cup of cooking liquid.

In a saucepan combine stevia, cornstarch and stir in reserved beet liquid, lemon juice and butter. Cook and stir until thickened and bubbling. Add beets; cook approximately 5 minutes more, constantly stirring.

Serves 4

Cabbage with Pecans

1 teaspoon instant beef bouillon granules
5 cups coarsely shredded cabbage
1 cup coarsely shredded carrot
2 tablespoons butter
½ cup sliced green onion
⅓ cup chopped pecans
1 teaspoon of dry mustard mixed with 1 teaspoon water

In a saucepan, heat bouillon granules in ¼ cup water to dissolve.

Add cabbage and carrots with onion and ¼ teaspoon pepper. Mix well and cook, uncovered over medium heat 5 to 10 minutes stirring once during cooking. Drain, if needed.

Combine butter, pecans and mustard then mix well. Add to vegetables and toss to mix.

Serves 6 to 8

Lemon Glazed Carrots

3 cups carrots in 1 inch pieces
⅜ teaspoon crushed stevia leaf powder
1 teaspoon cornstarch
¼ teaspoon ginger
¼ cup lemon juice
1 tablespoon butter

Cook carrots with 1 inch of boiling water for 10 to 15 minutes, drain and set aside.

In saucepan combine stevia, cornstarch and ginger with lemon juice and cook, stirring until thickened and bubbly, stir in butter.

Add carrots to saucepan and mix to coat.

Serves 6

Mint Peas

2 cups fresh peas, shelled
½ cup chopped green onion
3 tablespoons butter
2 tablespoons water
1 tablespoon finely chopped fresh mint or 1 teaspoon dried mint
⅛ teaspoon crushed stevia leaf powder
1 teaspoon lemon juice
¼ teaspoon dried rosemary

In a skillet, cook green onion in butter until tender. Add peas, water, mint, stevia, lemon juice and rosemary.

Cover and cook 10 to 12 minutes, peas should be tender.

Serves 4

Creamed Spinach

1 bunch of spinach, washed, cleaned and torn in pieces
1 tablespoon butter
½ cup coconut milk
1½ teaspoons cornstarch
Dash ground nutmeg

Cook spinach in a skillet with ½ cup water until wilted. Remove from heat but do not drain. Add butter to pan.

In a small bowl stir cornstarch into the coconut milk and add nutmeg. Add to spinach in skillet.

Return to heat and cook while stirring until thick and bubbly.

Serves 4

Vegetable Stir Fry

2 carrots cut into thin 3 inch sticks
2 cups green pea pods
2 cups green beans cut into 1-inch pieces
2 cups cauliflower, broken into bite sized florets
1 cup zucchini, sliced
1 medium onion cut in 1-inch pieces
1 ½ teaspoons cornstarch
2 tablespoons Bragg's amino acids
¼ teaspoon crushed stevia leaf powder
2 tablespoons extra virgin or cold pressed olive oil

In a covered saucepan, cook carrots and green beans in boiling water for 3 minutes. Add cauliflower florets, cover and cook another 2 minutes. Drain.

In a small bowl stir cornstarch into 2 tablespoons cold water, add stevia, Braggs and pepper, mix and set aside.

Preheat a wok or heavy skillet over high heat and add oil. Stir fry the onion in oil until tender and transparent, add carrots, beans, zucchini and cauliflower and stir-fry until crisp tender.

Move vegetables to sides of pan and add cornstarch mixture in center then mix in vegetables. Cook until thickened, about 3 to 4 minutes.

Serves 6

STANDARD WEIGHTS AND MEASUREMENTS

60 drops = 1 teaspoon
3 teaspoons = 1 tablespoon
4 tablespoons = ¼ cup
5 ⅓ tablespoons = ⅓ cup
8 tablespoons = ½ cup
10 ⅔ tablespoons = ⅔ cup
12 tablespoons = ¾ cup
16 tablespoons = 1 cup

1 tablespoon = ½ fluid ounce
1 cup = 8 fluid ounces
2 cups = 1 pint
4 cups = 1 quart
2 pints = 1 quart
4 quarts = 1 gallon
8 quarts = 1 peck
4 pecks = 1 bushel
1 pound = 16 ounces
One stick of butter weighs 4 ounces and is 1/2 cup
8 tablespoons = 1/4 pound butter
1 ounce = 28.35 grams
1 pound = 453.59 grams
1 gram = 0.035 ounces
1 kilogram = 2.2 pounds
1 tablespoon = 14.79 millimeters
1 cup = 236.6 milliliters
1 quart = 946.4 milliliters
1.06 quarts = 1 liter

INDEX

978-0-595-40055-3
0-595-40055-8

Printed in the United States
131136LV00002B/172/A